MACHINE EMBROIDERY
Wild & Wacky

Linda Turner Griepentrog and Rebecca Kemp Brent

©2006 Linda Turner Griepentrog and Rebecca Kemp Brent
Published by

 krause publications
An Imprint of F+W Publications

700 East State Street • Iola, WI 54990-0001
715-445-2214 • 888-457-2873

Our toll-free number to place an order or obtain
a free catalog is (800) 258-0929.

The following registered trademark terms, publications and companies appear in this publication:
AMACO®, Amazing Designs®, Angelina®, Baby Lock®, Bernina®, Blumenthal™ Craft Crafter's Images™,
Brilliance™, Brother®, Buzz Tools®, BuzzEdit™, BuzzSize™, BuzzXplore™, The C-Thru® Ruler Company, Cactus
Punch®, Calico Crossroads®, Chenille Brush™, Click-n-Craft®, Clotilde®, Cover-Up™, Crafter's Pick™ The
Ultimate!® Glue, Creative Design®, Déjà Views®, DMC®, Embroidery Central®, Embroidery Resource™, Fabric
Café®, Fiber Etch®, Fiskars®, Glue Dots®, Green Sneakers™, Hollywood Lights™, Hoop-It-All™, Husqvarna®
Viking®, K-Lace®, Kaleidoscope Kreator™, Kandi Kane™, Klaer International™, Kreate-a-Lope®, Lick & Stick™,
Lite Steam-A-Seam 2®, Martha Pullen®, Mylar®, NU-Foam®, Poly-fil®, Puffy Foam™, Quick Rust™ Steel,
RibbonFloss®, ScrapSmart™, Silkpaint®, Singer®, Smart Needle®, SolarActive™, Steam-A-Seam 2®, Sulky® of
America, Textile Tool™, UltraTwist™, The Vintage Workshop®, Walnut Hollow®, The Warm™ Company

The following design credits apply: Title page: Brother, Ultimate Embroidery Designs, Birds 1;
Table of Contents: Cactus Punch, Snap It Up

Library of Congress Catalog Number: 2006929414

ISBN-13: 978-0-89689-277-4
ISBN-10: 0-89689-277-8

Edited by Sarah Brown
Designed by Elizabeth Krogwold

Printed in China

Acknowledgments

We'd like to thank several people and companies for the reality of this book.

First, thank you to Jeanine Twigg for the expert digitizing and support she's given us with the designs on the enclosed CD-ROM. Her embroidery experience has been most valuable. The "Embroidery Machine Essentials" book series she wrote for Krause Publications offers great basic information from which we've gone over to the more wacky side.

Special thanks, as well, go to Annette Gentry Bailey, editor of Creative Machine Embroidery magazine and author of "Machine Embroidery on Paper," also from Krause Publications, for her inspiration and encouragement. She allows us both to play in the pages of the magazine on a regular basis, and is responsible for introducing us to each other.

Linda would like to thank fellow sewers/ writers/embroiderers Pam Archer, Stephanie Goddard, Janet Klaer and Pauline Richards who oohed and aahed at some of the samples and project photos and gave encouragement that the book writing task was indeed attainable. In addition, kudos go to her husband Keith, who gave unending support to the book writing process and checked in frequently to see how things were going (more likely it was, "When will this thing be done?"). Mini-thanks go to Riley and Buckley, aka "the fur children," who put up with Mom's endless hours at the computer when she should have been out throwing toys for retrieval.

As we surveyed friends for wild and wacky things, first to mind was Nicky Bookout who was doing weirdness before most of us even thought about it. Thanks for sharing!

Rebecca would like to thank Linda first of all, for inviting her to be part of this fun. Thanks also to her children, Patricia and Jonathan, for their unending encouragement and understanding, and to Mom and Dad who have been her biggest fans for a long time. She'd be remiss not to mention Paddy and Ramona, who have contributed all they could by sleeping on idle fabric (or the computer keyboard), purring all the while.

Many thanks to Husqvarna Viking and Brother for the loan of wonderful embroidery machines and to RNK Distributing for all the stabilizers used to keep all our book samples pucker-free.

We'd also like to give our appreciation to the companies who supported us with products, designs and samples to share with you. Those companies are listed in the Resources on page 124 and credited with their photos throughout the text. Each book photo also has a design credit so you can duplicate the samples. All designs are current at publication. Without their support, this book would not have been possible.

Table of Contents

CD-ROM Contents

Introduction

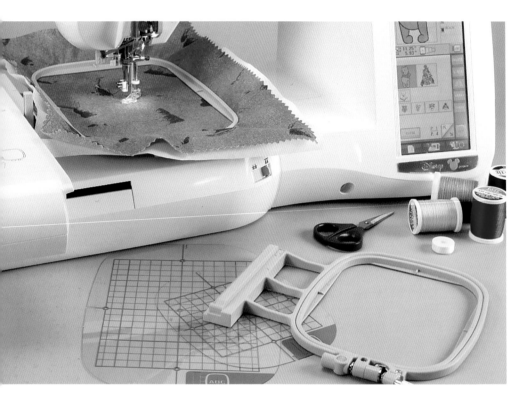

planned these designs to encourage your success as you explore new media and techniques. Never ones to stop with just one use, we also offer plenty of ideas for using each design — just in case you need inspiration.

We have made the assumption that you have basic machine embroidery skills before you expand your horizons to have fun with us. If you're not certain of that, we suggest that you read Jeanine Twigg's "Embroidery Machine Essentials" and "More Embroidery Machine Essentials," both published by Krause Publications, to reacquaint yourself with the basics.

"Machine Embroidery Wild & Wacky" is a clever name for the silliness that we believe can overwhelm you once you've mastered the basics of machine embroidery!

We give you permission to think outside the hoop and try those things that you perhaps think about in the middle of the night — like embroidering on metal, wood or paper.

Those haunting questions of "I wonder what would happen if ... ?" and "Hmm, how could I embroider on ... ?" can now be resolved without harm to you or to your embroidery machine.

We have figured out how to stitch on some very unusual things — some funny and some more serious — and have created original designs for you to play with, too. This book's projects and samples include a mix of commercially available embroidery designs and the original motifs found on the enclosed multi-format CD-ROM. We

Why would you want to embroider on some of life's oddities? Linda's answer is "because you can," and Rebecca's is simply "Why not?" There is more to embroidery than putting a design on a sweatshirt or denim shirt, and this book will challenge you to go beyond your current comfort level and have fun doing it.

We've stitched on all the things we've written about and the machines are still running! Perhaps we're naïve and don't know any better, but we'd prefer to think that we could open up a whole new world to you. We teamed up together to write this book because we each have different embroidery orientations but the same wacky sense of experimentation and curiosity. We encourage you to play along with us!

Stitching Everything
From A to 3

Linda Visnaw, Threads & Ink Together

Get ready to think outside the box (or would that be "embroidery hoop?") to embroider on lots of unusual things. It's safe, sane and lots of fun!

Additions

Addition — that simple, basic math skill — comes in handy when personalizing embroidery motifs. Almost anything can be added to your stitching, depending on the use of the final project and its required care. There are several ways to add things to your embroidery motifs.

Enclosed CD-ROM, Gumball

Pompoms add dimension to this child's Gumball Apron project. Find the project instructions and the embroidery design on the enclosed CD-ROM.

Substitutions

Sue Lord, Doily Belles

Cactus Punch, Petite Petals

Embroidables, Doggie Collection

Cactus Punch, Country Critters Appliqué

Using embroidery software, edit out a section of stitching or simply skip over it in the stitching process, leaving a visible gap in the design. Put your creative juices to work and imagine all the things that could fill the gap! Tassels, fringe, pompoms, scrapbook findings and pre-made trims are all fair game, as are a host of other notions like bells, buckles, ribbons, raffia, bows, pre-made flowers, feathers, etc.

Add-Ons

Rowena Charlton Designs, Kids' Activity Panel

Some additions, like a 3-D dog collar on Fido, can also make the design interactive.

Husqvarna Viking, Faces

Trims and fringes sold by the yard or as individual pieces make wonderful additions to create hair above embroidered faces.

Enclosed CD-ROM, Basket

Embroidery can form the basis of a large or more complex motif by adding details to make it even larger or more interesting. These additions can be placed outside the embroidered area or on top of a portion of the actual embroidery stitching.

Accents

Enclosed CD-ROM, LindaCar

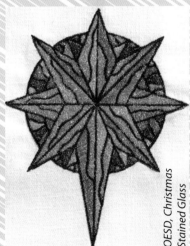

Hot-fix jewels and metal findings are perfect accents for embroidery motifs.

OESD, FM283

Charms, beads, metallic findings and scrapbook findings can be used as accents for embroidery on top of the stitching but not covering it completely. The base stitching shows through or around the accents.

Getting It On

Depending on what's being added to the embroidery, there are several ways to attach the findings. Hand sewing works well for things like beads, tags, charms, etc., where there is a hole for threading. Soft findings like tassels and trims can also be attached by hand or even with machine stitching. Matching or invisible thread helps to minimize stitches showing for the attachment process.

Depending on the project use, glue can also be used for some additions. Check the label for compatible care instructions if the project will be washed or dry cleaned. Some glues are permanent, others are not. Other attachment options include ribbons, chain loops, ties, etc.

Just A Thought

Puttin' on the Glitz

Stitch an ordinary design, then add texture and sparkle with a sprinkle of glitter. Choose glitter and adhesive designed for textile applications for the best results. Match the glitter color to the thread, or use a light coat of clear or iridescent glitter over an entire motif.

OESD, Christmas Stained Glass

Enclosed CD-ROM, FabBord/Kandi Corp., Iron-Ons

Iron-ons add sparkle to this easy-to-embroider Border Belt project. Find the project instructions and the embroidery design on the enclosed CD-ROM.

Iron-Ons

Iron-on accents come in a wide variety of shapes, sizes and finishes, and they're the perfect way to add a little sparkle and pizzazz to your embroidery motifs. Look for metallics, crystals, rhinestones, pearls, sequins and other novelties.

When applying heat-sensitive shapes, be sure your background fabric can tolerate the heat needed for permanent application. If in doubt, try a sample before planning your embroidery to include iron-on accents. Accents can be applied on top of machine embroidery, or adjacent to it. Each piece is coated with heat-activated adhesive on the under surface. Use a heated applicator tool to apply individual pieces using a tip size that corresponds to the accent size. Applicator wands come with tips in multiple sizes.

To use, pre-heat the tool as directed, then pick up the accent and position it on or next to your embroidery. Hold the wand vertically and press for up to 15 seconds to adhere the piece. The heat-activated glue will adhere the accent to the fabric; contact time will vary depending on the size of the piece. The applicator tool becomes very hot during use. Avoid touching any metal parts and store the tool in a stand when it's not in use. Allow the tool to cool before storing.

Kandi Kane

Kandi Corp. photo

Appliqués

Enclosed CD-ROM, BearApp

Don't forget the simple addition of another fabric layer. Appliqués, especially in unusual or textured fabrics, add a great designer touch — and cut embroidery time significantly!

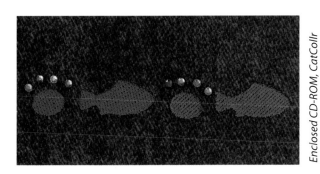

Enclosed CD-ROM, CatCollr

Enclosed CD-ROM, BearApp

Enclosed CD-ROM, FabricSW

Why not experiment with appliqué on paper, too? Either trim the applied paper with scissors or moisten it just outside the stitching line, then carefully tear away the excess to leave a feathered edge.

Angelina

Angelina is a wonderful ingredient for a book about the freewheeling, fun side of digitized machine embroidery. It's sparkly, creative and unique. Made from polyester fibers, Angelina is washable and soft. It comes in two forms, regular and heat-bondable, and a wide range of colors, including metallics and iridescents.

Sadia's Designs, Farsi II

Making Magic

Heat-bondable Angelina is the most useful form for machine embroidery. It comes packaged in deceptively small plastic bags — a little goes a long way! In addition to the Angelina fibers, you will need two non-stick pressing sheets or parchment paper, and an iron.

1. Pull a bit of fiber from its bag and separate it with your fingers, allowing stray fibers to fall onto one non-stick sheet.

2. Arrange the fibers randomly on the sheet, adding more as desired to make a piece large enough for your project. The fibers can be layered thickly for a sturdy Angelina sheet, or left thin and wispy to create a delicate overlay. Use one color or a combination to suit your fancy. For more color possibilities, blend heat-bondable and regular Angelina fibers.

3. When the arrangement is satisfactory, cover the Angelina with the second non-stick sheet. Press with a warm iron; the silk or polyester setting is appropriate on most irons, but it's best to test a small area first. Use a quick, firm pressure to bond the Angelina fibers between the non-stick sheets.

4. Turn the Angelina over and press again from the other side to complete the bond.

Enclosed CD-ROM, LindaCar

Angelina bonds only to itself, so it will not stick to the pressing sheets, and stray fibers will not bond to the ironing surface. Quick pressure will create a fluffy sheet with wispy fibers that may be pulled away from the surface. More time spent on bonding makes a firmer sheet that is flatter, glossier and less likely to separate. Even for a firm bond, press the Angelina for only a few seconds. Overheating, whether with too much heat or too much dwell time, will distort the color and make the sheet crisp.

While Angelina does not bond to other surfaces, it is possible to trap bits and pieces of other materials within the Angelina sheet (confetti, string, paper, etc.).

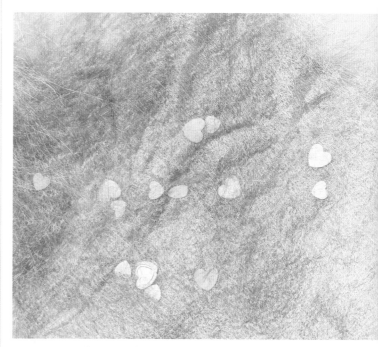

Trap sequins between layers of Angelina for added glitz and shimmer.

1. Begin with a thin layer of heat-bondable Angelina fibers on one non-stick sheet. Add bits of relatively flat items that can be stitched through and will not be melted by the iron.

2. Cover with a second thin Angelina layer.

3. Top with the second non-stick sheet and press to fuse the fibers.

To create a sturdier Angelina sheet, place the fused material between two layers of fine chiffon or tulle, or between fabric and a sheer overlay. The sparkly finish will still be visible, and the thin fabric overlayer will protect the Angelina.

Using Angelina for Machine Embroidery

For machine embroidery, Angelina can be used as an appliqué material or as a base fabric for embroidery.

Angelina as an Appliqué

Treat a fused sheet of Angelina as you would any other appliqué material. Position it as required for the embroidery motif, stitch the appliqué shape, and trim away the excess. Finish stitching the embroidery design, and the appliqué is complete.

Angelina is a wonderful material for dimensional appliqué pieces. The slight stiffness of well-fused Angelina gives the dimensional pieces enough body to stand away from the background fabric. The sparkly fiber is ideal for dragonfly wings, fairy costumes, jewelry and other fanciful dimensional creations.

Design By Dawn, Crystal Embroidery featuring Snow Lady Designs

To fashion a dimensional appliqué, create a moderately thick, sturdy Angelina sheet large enough to fill your embroidery hoop. Wind a bobbin to match the needle thread. Stitch the dimensional pieces on the Angelina, then cut out and position on the embroidered base as directed by the dimensional design's digitizer.

If the Angelina alone will not support the appliqué stitches, back the fused sheet with water-soluble stabilizer before hooping. Stitch and trim the designs, then rinse away the stabilizer. Lay the pieces flat to dry on a towel. The appliqués can be pressed lightly if they curl when wet, but do not iron them dry, since the extra heat will cause a color change.

Angelina as an Embroidery Base

Angelina works well as a base for openwork embroidery designs.

Back the Angelina with cut-away stabilizer or paper to help support the embroidery stitches. Choose an embroidery motif that will allow the sparkly surface to show. Redwork and outline-only motifs are ideal. Layer the Angelina over quilt batting to create a padded surface with a slightly sculptured appearance.

Just A Thought

Making an Outline

Occasionally, the outline stitching on an embroidered motif doesn't appear exactly where it should be. Some fill stitches may find their way outside the outline, or it may appear as if something has slipped during the stitching process, either due to poor hooping techniques, fabric pulling, or the wrong choice of stabilizer.

Rather than throwing the stitchout away, search your art supplies for a permanent pen with a narrow tip to correct the situation. A .05 mm tip works well for coloring individual stitches to match their adjoining areas inconspicuously. Look for the pens in sets or individually at your craft, scrapbooking or fabric store.

Keep in mind that this super-sleuth technique works only when there is minimal displacement and when the thread color is darker than the adjacent stitch background.

Bobbinwork

Have you ever looked at a wonderful heavy thread and wondered how to incorporate it into your machine embroidery? Look at the work from a different angle — upside down! By winding the heavy thread on a bobbin and hooping the project with the fabric wrong-side up and stabilizer on top, you can stitch with a variety of unconventional threads.

YLI, DigiBobbE Collection I Ornamental Swirls

Working with heavy threads in the bobbin is best accomplished with adjustments to the bobbin tension. A tiny screw on the bobbin case turns to increase or decrease pressure on the case's spring, creating more or less drag on the thread as it passes beneath the spring on its way out of the bobbin case. Miniscule adjustments can make a big difference in stitch quality, and it can be difficult to return the screw to its proper position, so machine manufacturers discourage users from making adjustments to the bobbin tension.

The best option is to purchase an extra bobbin case to use exclusively for bobbinwork. Mark the case clearly with nail polish or a permanent marker to distinguish it from the standard bobbin case used for other embroidery and sewing.

Find the Bobbinwork Evening Bag project instructions and the embroidery design on the enclosed CD-ROM.

Sometimes bobbinwork can be created without tension adjustments, or by bypassing the bobbin tension completely. To bypass the tension, simply insert the bobbin into the case without threading the heavy thread through the tension spring, or use special features available on some machines (check your owner's manual). Insert the bobbin case into the machine, pull up the bobbin thread and proceed as usual. Bobbinwork created with no tension on the bobbin thread will have a loopy, free-form texture very different from tensioned stitches.

This photo shows two identical motifs. The sample on the left shows normal bobbin tension; on the right, the bobbin tension has been bypassed.

YLI, DigiBobbE Collection I Ornamental Swirls

Thread Tales

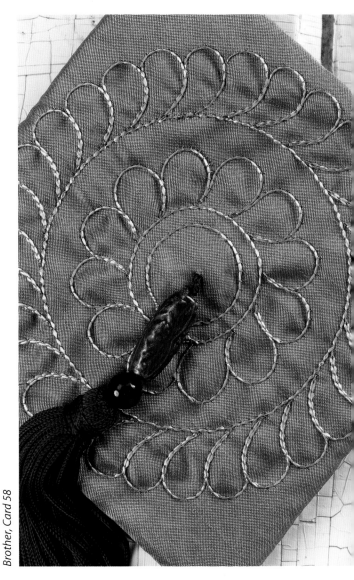

Brother, Card 58

Threads for bobbinwork run the gamut from metallic fiber-laced decorative serger yarns to narrow silk ribbons. Look for fibers flexible enough to wind around the bobbin and pass through the hook that forms the stitches. Begin with threads and yarns intended for machine use to establish experience with the technique, then branch out to other threads, yarns and fine ribbons.

Silk ribbon for bobbinwork is generally 2 mm wide. These ribbons, packaged and marketed primarily for hand embroidery, are very soft and are easily gathered into place by the machine stitches.

Winding a bobbin with heavy thread is little different from ordinary bobbin winding. In some cases, it may be necessary to bypass one or more thread guides so the heavy thread feeds smoothly onto the bobbin. Use a slow winding speed, if possible, and be sure the thread winds evenly in a series of parallel wraps. Winding the bobbin by hand is an alternative if machine winding is unsatisfactory, and may be the best option for filling silk-ribbon bobbins.

The needle thread will be almost hidden in the finished work, but may appear as tiny dots between stitches. Use a regular sewing or embroidery thread in the needle, or select an invisible sewing thread. The invisible thread, with its tendency to stretch and relax, may actually contribute to attractive bobbinwork by increasing the needle-thread tension. For colored threads, match the needle and bobbin threads for the most invisible join, or choose a needle thread that matches the fabric for unnoticeable stitching on the project wrong side.

Design Decisions

Bobbinwork embroidery designs should be outline-only motifs, lines or swirls. Look for specially digitized motifs or try quilting designs. Choose stitch paths that have few, if any, retraced stitches, since the heavy thread looks less attractive if allowed to pile up.

Stitch a sample with the threads and fabric you will use to spot any problems in using a particular design:

- If the tie-off stitches create an unattractive knot, they can be skipped or edited out in software.
- If the needle thread shows in curved areas of the design, tighten the needle tension or lower the bobbin tension.
- If the decorative bobbin thread has a loose, sloppy appearance, increase the bobbin tension by tightening the bobbin-case screw.

Upside Down Embroidery

1. After winding the bobbin with heavy thread, load the bobbin into the machine and thread the needle.

2. Lay the fabric face-down on the outer hoop and cover with stabilizer. Lightweight cut-away stabilizer or water- or heat-soluble stabilizers are good options, since the stress of removing a tear-away stabilizer may distort the stitches.

3. Insert the inner hoop and tighten, then place the hoop on the machine.

4. If your machine has an automatic thread cutter, turn it off for bobbinwork.

5. Move the needle to the first stitch position and draw the bobbin thread to the top of the work. Grasp and hold both thread tails as you begin to stitch.

6. When the final stitch is complete, raise the needle and presser foot and remove the hoop.

7. Cut the needle and bobbin threads, leaving a 3" tail.

8. Use a large-eye needle or fine crochet hook to draw the bobbin thread to the fabric wrong side and secure it by knotting with the needle thread or by taking a few hand stitches over the thread tails where they will be hidden on the project right side. Repeat the process at each end of any jump stitches within the design.

Buttons

Smart Needle,
Cute Buttons

We often think of buttons only as functional closures, but there's a whole new world out there when you look at them as embroidery accents. Button companies have hundreds of fun offerings to tempt creative sewers. Check out the novelty buttons in the apparel section of your local fabric store, but also visit craft and scrapbooking stores for even more offerings. Some button companies have coordinated groupings of buttons bagged by themes, like summer fun, back to school, etc., and each grouping contains multiple button accents.

The Hole Story

Two types of buttons are available — sew-through and shank. Sew-through buttons have holes in them — two, three, four or more, depending on the button. To incorporate them into your embroidery motifs, you can sew them on by hand or by machine.

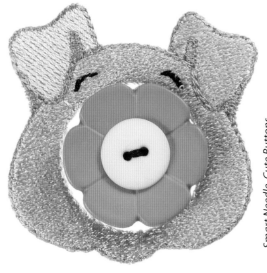

Smart Needle, Cute Buttons

Smart Needle, Cute Buttons

Sew-through buttons can be stacked for added interest — just line up the holes and stitch through multiple buttons at one pass. A drop of glue or double-stick tape can help to hold stacked buttons in place for the sewing process. Be sure to let the glue dry before you sew! Mix colors and/or textures to create the perfect embroidery accent.

Amazing Designs, French Country

Sew-through buttons lie flat against your embroidery motif and you can use decorative threads to attach them by hand. They can also be sewn or tied on using narrow ribbon, novelty threads or tiny trims, as long as they fit into a needle and the needle fits through the hole in the button. Add beads, twist threads or knot the thread on top of the button for added interest, and mix the attachment threads for texture.

Loop Lingo

Shank buttons have a metal or molded loop protruding from the back, allowing the button to sit above the fabric surface when used as a garment closure. For embroidery accents, it's best to remove the shank so the button can sit flat against the stitching and not tilt. Use pliers, wire cutters or a specially designed button shank remover tool to clip off the protrusion. A drop of craft glue will hold the flat-back button in place on your embroidery.

If you prefer not to trim the shank, make a small eyelet, tiny buttonhole or a tiny slit (use seam sealant to prevent fraying) in the embroidery at the button center positioning, then push the shank through and anchor the button on the fabric underside. This allows the button to be removed for washing or cleaning.

Just A Thought

Keep it Cool

Don't hoop recently-pressed fabric while it is still warm. Creases will set more firmly, resulting in hoop marks that are hard to remove.

Embroidery Fun

Most buttons can be painted if you need more patterning — experiment with good quality craft paint to add dots, stripes or other designs to solid-color buttons. Add a protective coating if the button will be washed or dry-cleaned.

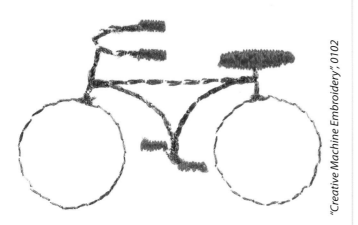

"Creative Machine Embroidery", 0102

Amazing Designs, Heirloom Floral

Some embroidery motifs are designed specifically to incorporate buttons and they leave space in the stitching for the button placement. Look for button placement indicators with outlined areas, or even a stitched X to mark the spot; others leave a rough space for the button.

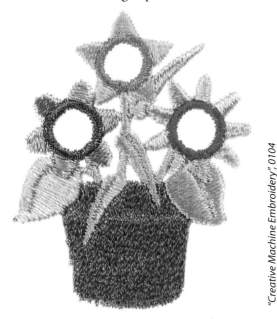

"Creative Machine Embroidery", 0104

If the embroidery is planned to include buttons, be sure to note the size intended, as you may need to re-size the design to fit a given button. Don't let motifs not planned for buttons deter your creative mind. Buttons can be placed on top of stitched areas!

Buttons can also substitute for a color within a design — just leave the color unstitched, either by removing it in an editing program, or by skipping that color during the embroidery process.

Cover-Ups

Embroidery motifs can also be used to make covered buttons. Double-check the size of the design compared to the button your project calls for and use embroidery software or on-screen editing to change the design size.

Forms for covering your own buttons come in metal and plastic and can be flat or dome shaped. Look for sizes from ¼" to 2½". Think about them not only for use as buttons, but also as jewelry, pins, pendants and holiday ornaments. Embroidered buttons are also great home décor accents for pillows, tie-backs and tassel toppers. For more ideas, see J — Jewelry on page 56 and the Tile Pillow project on the book CD-ROM.

Embroider the motif on the button fabric, then make a see-through circle template using the pattern that comes with the button form to draw the shape on the fabric right side. Center the motif on the button, unless you want to create a purposeful asymmetric look. If you opt for this artistic touch, be sure it looks like you planned it and not that the fabric slipped while you were trying to cover the button!

To help keep the motif centered during the covering process, use a small piece of double-stick tape on the button front to hold the embroidered fabric in place, or spray the button cover with temporary adhesive.

If your button embroidery is on a light color or loosely woven fabric, consider leaving the stabilizer under the stitching to prevent the button form surface from shining through.

A Bit of Stitch, Spring Button Covers

Just A Thought

Sew Man, HR-129

Pressing Thoughts

It's a good idea to press your finished embroidery from the wrong side. If you press on the right side, any "gunk" that might be on the sole plate of your iron can adhere to the raised embroidery surface, causing permanent damage. Better yet, be sure to clean your iron sole plate on a regular basis!

Chenille

Enclosed CD-ROM, RattleLo, RattleUp and Chenille

Chenille is made by stacking layers of fabrics, stitching parallel channels and slashing through all but the lowest layer. The fabrics are then washed and brushed to encourage fraying, giving the final piece a soft, fuzzy appearance created by the blending of the various layers. Making your own chenilled fabric using the embroidery machine allows you to customize coordinating fabrics for your project, then use your fuzzy swatches in a number of ways.

Make your own chenille for this baby quilt using the embroidery designs and following the instructions on the enclosed CD-ROM. Our chenille baby quilt project uses four chenilled fabrics as the rattle top appliqué, adding a great sense of dimension and coordinating with the fleece colors used in the quilt.

Fabrics

The best chenilling fabrics are those made from natural fibers or blends of them — cotton, silk and linen work well, as does rayon. The looser the weave, the more fraying occurs.

Fabrics used in chenille can be prints or solids, and even the ugliest fabrics often add charm to the final fuzzies, as they blend with others during the fraying process. Play with colors on a test sample before committing to a color sequence — test-wash the stitched piece to see what happens to it and be sure it looks like what you envisioned. The same colors arranged in a different order look totally different.

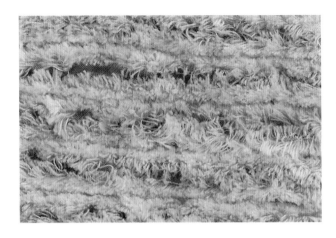

These fabric colors produced both chenille versions when they were arranged in a different stacking order.

Fabric Café Chenille Brush

Chenille brushes have stiff bristles to help the fabric edges fray.

The Process

To create chenille using the embroidery machine, use the Chenille design on the enclosed CD-ROM to stitch perfectly parallel rows of stitching.

1. Stack four to six layers of fabric on the straight grain and hoop them together. No stabilizer is needed for this process, as the multiple layers of fabrics keep any puckering at bay.

2. Stitch the design and unhoop the fabric. Remove the perimeter basting line, and trim the square about 1" larger all around than the stitched area.

3. Starting at the edge, slide sharp scissors blades between the base layer and upper layers and cut between the stitched channels. Do not cut the base layer!

4. Serge the perimeter to prevent excess fraying during the washing process.

5. Toss the stitched and slashed sample in with a load of laundry (similar colors of course) and let the washer do its work of fraying. For the protection of other items, put the stitched sample in a mesh bag, and be sure to clean out the lint filter after washing, as some fabrics create lots of lint in the fraying process. When you remove the sample from the washer, it should appear slightly to significantly frayed, depending on the fabric selection.

6. Before putting the sample in the dryer, brush it with a wire brush to encourage further fraying. You can buy a chenille brush designed specifically for this purpose. Don't hesitate to brush vigorously for the best fraying.

7. Put the chenille sample in the dryer with the same load of laundry you washed it with, and dry thoroughly.

Uses

The chenilled sample can be used like any other embroidered fabric. Combine it with an appliqué motif, use it for only portions of an embroidered appliqué, or stitch the raw-edge squares to a base fabric for an all-over pattern of color.

Instead of making freestanding squares of chenille, layer fabrics for an entire project and stitch the embroidered square over only portions of the project, then wash and dry to create chenilled patterning throughout.

Rebecca Says

For another look, add conventional embroidery or appliqué on top of chenilled fabric. Begin by stitching and slashing the chenille channels as directed above, but don't wash or brush just yet. Cover the chenille layers with a lightweight, water-soluble stabilizer and embroider the motif. Filled designs or appliqués work best, as they are less likely to become lost in the chenille texture. Finally, wash, dry and brush the chenille to complete the texturing process.

Coloring

If the scent of a new box of crayons or the sight of an artist's palette adds a thrill to your day, try combining machine embroidery with coloring techniques for the best of both worlds.

Experiment with coloring using the embroidery design and following the instructions for this card on the enclosed CD-ROM.

Enclosed CD-ROM, Iris/WCorner

Design Decisions

Brother, Card 65

Look for motifs with plenty of open area to fill with color. Appliqué designs are a possibility; the simple appliqué shapes create a canvas for blending colors or adding texture with rubbing techniques. Substitute paints, markers or crayons for the appliqué fabric.

Redwork designs are also good choices for coloring. Consider using black or dark gray thread, or even sepia brown or metallic gold instead of red for stitching the outlines.

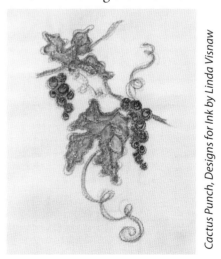

Cactus Punch, Designs for Ink by Linda Visnaw

You can even include painted or inked color in designs not intended for coloring. Leave out one or all of the fill colors, stitching only the outline. Fill the empty areas with your choice of coloring techniques.

Paints

Many different textile paints are available in craft and discount stores — look for metallic, opaque and translucent options. Use them to fill open design areas with a flat wash of color, or experiment with different brushes and painting techniques to create textured designs. Some paints need to be heat set before washing, either with an iron or by tumble drying. Be sure to check the manufacturer's instructions for specifics.

Crayons

One of the easiest and most accessible coloring possibilities is crayon art. Crayons are an excellent choice for children's coloring projects, but adult artists enjoy them, too.

Some crayons are specifically intended for coloring fabric. They may be the best choice for projects that need durability to withstand repeated wash-and-wear cycles. Choose crayons that you can apply directly to the fabric for greatest control. Fabric crayons that are applied to paper first and transferred to the fabric with a hot iron can be used for backgrounds or free-form techniques.

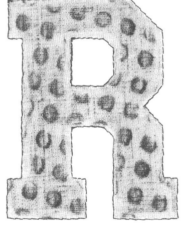

Brother, Card 37

Place the fabric on a textured surface (window screening or embossing/texturing plates from paper crafting supplies, for example) and rub crayons across the fabric for textured fill designs.

Even ordinary crayons can be used to color fabric. Look for quality brands that contain a high proportion of pigment to wax. Experiment with light and heavy color fills. Try packing an open area with lines, squiggles or crosshatching. Press the fabric between paper towels after coloring to set the color and remove excess wax.

Markers

Brother, Card 56

Check the craft and scrapbooking aisles at your favorite store for a variety of markers. Some are specifically intended for fabrics, but others may be permanent on fabrics as well. Gel pens are one example; their opaque inks are permanent and visible even on dark fabrics.

Use a light touch when coloring with markers. More color can be added later, if desired. Marker-colored designs look more artistic when there is variation in the color. Experiment with blending different colors to create highlights and shadows. Brush markers are useful for filling large areas with color, but avoid the temptation to scrub the marker repeatedly over the same area. Instead, use stroke-and-lift motions to apply some color over the area, *then* draw details with a hard-tip pen.

Tips

- *Wash and dry the fabric or garment before coloring to remove factory finishes. Don't use fabric softener, which is designed to coat the fibers and creates a barrier between the fabric and the color. Spray starch may also inhibit the color/fabric bond, so use it lightly on the wrong side only.*
- *Coloring is easier on stable fabric. Try leaving the fabric in the hoop, or leave a fusible stabilizer in place while you color. If the stabilizer has been removed, replace it with freezer paper or stabilizer while coloring.*
- *To allow more room for coloring, enlarge an outline motif so there is more space for embellishment. Add details with markers to avoid an empty look.*

What to Do

BAROQUE

Calico Crossroads, CD402

Cactus Punch, Designs for Ink by Linda Visnaw

Your colored embroideries can be used for projects from home décor to apparel. Consider the colorfastness and durability of the chosen coloring method when deciding on the embroidery's end use. In general, fabric markers and textile crayons or paints are durable enough for repeated washings.

If your project is colored with watercolor pencils or regular crayons, use it for home décor projects or mount and frame it. For an easy finish, center the embroidery on a self-adhesive mounting board and place it in a purchased frame, with or without an additional mat.

One more possibility is to stitch outline designs on a child's T-shirt. Wrap the embroidered shirt with a package of washable crayons or markers for a gift the child can color, wear, wash and color — again and again!

Dimensional Embroidery

$\mathcal{W}$ho says embroidery has to be flat? Although it's a goal we aspire to for most stitching, there are times when flat stitching on a base just doesn't work.

Consider things that you can't really embroider on, but you'd like to add a touch of stitchery to them — shoes, books, pre-made items like cell phone holders and water bottle cases — there's no way to stitch on these items. What if you want wiggly ears on an animal, or a free-standing corsage? Dimensional embroidery techniques to the rescue …

Cactus Punch, Gingerbread House

Husqvarna Viking, Pop-Up Pals

Most any design can be adapted to 3-D embroidery if it has some kind of outline stitch around a filled-in area, or an outline by itself. Some designs are digitized specifically to become dimensional pieces, others are not.

Covering Your Bases

Free-standing designs need to be stitched on a firm base — stabilizer, organza, felt, wool, suede, etc. — to help maintain the design integrity and to create a non-raveling edge. An additional removable stabilizer can be used for the technique, but in some instances none is needed.

For the lightest-weight work, use organza as a base. It can be totally covered with stitching or show through the embroidery. Multiple layers of organza add firmness and also offer the option of stacking more than one color for variation within an embroidered piece.

Embroidery

Choose as small a hoop as possible to hold the fabric tautly without stretching. For flower petals or multiple leaves, use software to group the motifs for fewer hoopings. Use matching thread in the bobbin to avoid show-through and discoloration on sheer fabrics or where both sides of the embroidery will show. This is especially important for satin stitch outlines.

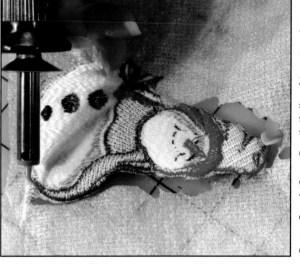

Cactus Punch, Snow Family/Sulky of America photo

After the embroidery is complete, use small, sharp scissors to cut very close to the outline stitching, but be careful not to cut *through* the stitching. If the base fabric is a synthetic, like nylon organza or stabilizer, use a hot knife or stenciling tool to sear the edges. It's easy to melt a bit too far and end up with scorched edges or melted threads, so practice this technique on scraps before you attempt the real deal.

These dimensional fruits were embroidered first, then assembled.

Rowena Charlton Designs, Tutti-Frutti

Assembly

Some dimensional pieces are finished once they're trimmed; others require some assembly to take shape. Some embroidery motifs even include the assembly as the final step of the digitized design.

If you're making flowers with assorted petals and leaves, use a small base of faux suede or felt and start layering the components (leaves and flower petals) from the base up, stitching each firmly to the base at the center. Start with the largest leaves/petals at the base and build up to smaller ones. For flower centers, use ribbon, beads, yarn or buttons to cover the joinings.

Use pins, hook-and-loop tape, pin backs or sewing to anchor free-standing embroideries to the project, garment or accessory to allow for easy removal prior to laundering.

Orange, OESD, FL290; Blue, Brother, Card 47, courtesy of Creative Machine Embroidery

Create a collection of colorful butterflies without catching a single one.

Unembroiderables

To attach free-standing motifs to things like shoes and other unembroiderables, use a fabric or craft glue that will not soak through the embroidery. Depending on the size of the motif, use glue only on the edges if it is to be secured flat on the item's surface, or use glue only in the middle to maintain dimensionality.

Another option is to sew the embroidery to the base. On fabric shoes, reach inside with the needle and thread to stitch through the upper shoe surface.

A Bit of Stitch, Applied Bugs

Needle Note

As the needle penetrates an item to embroider it, friction develops with each penetration. Couple that friction-generated heat with an adhesive stabilizer and it can be a sticky situation. The needle can develop gumminess and cause the thread to break. To help prevent this snafu, use a titanium-coated needle in the machine. It minimizes heat build-up and the subsequent problems that occur from it.

Embossing

Who would have thought that a heavily-embroidered motif could be used just like a rubber stamp to emboss fabric?

Surface Appeal

Selecting the right base fabric is important to hold the impression of the embroidered motif. Silk, acetate or rayon velvet (or a blend of these fibers) is the best base for embossing, as the image melds permanently into the surface. These fiber combinations can be dry cleaned and the image will remain clear.

Although some other velvet fiber combinations may work, avoid nylon and polyester bases, and of course velvets labeled as washable, because the embossed images will disappear during washing or steam pressing.

Tip

Reusing an embroidered motif for embossing may flatten it and subsequent impressions will not be as strong. If you plan to emboss lots of images, stitch out multiple motifs to use for clearer impressions.

Use embroidered lace motifs to emboss velvet.

Martha Pullen, Martha's Antique Lace Motifs

Im-press

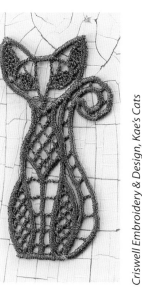

Criswell Embroidery & Design, Kae's Cats

1. If your iron has steam holes, purchase a protective cover to avoid replicating the hole pattern on your project.

2. Choose a design with a strong, dense stitching pattern; free-standing lace motif patterns work well, as do other motifs with raised surfaces. Embroider the motif with 12-weight or 30-weight thread; cotton or polyester threads hold up better to heat than rayons.

3. Place the motif right-side up on a very hard pressing surface, like plywood or a block of hardwood. A padded ironing board will not work because it is too soft. Set the iron for high heat (test on a fabric sample first to avoid damage) and a dry setting. Some fabrics may require using a press cloth to avoid scorching.

4. Determine the location of the impression and mark it on the wrong side of the velvet with chalk. Use a small spray bottle to spritz the velvet wrong side in the embossable area. The fabric should be damp, but not wet.

5. Place the fabric right-side down over the embroidered motif, centering the design under the placement marking.

6. Push the iron down firmly for 15 to 20 seconds. Don't slide the iron or the image may blur.

7. When the embossing process is complete, the damp fabric should be dry and you should see the embroidered motif details on the fabric right side.

Bad Luck?

Criswell Embroidery & Design, Antique Reflections

Uneven embossing occurs with uneven iron pressure — get creative and cover the problem area with beads, ribbons, etc.

If the embroidered motif design did not transfer to the velvet, it may not be heavily embroidered enough to work with this technique. Try using a heavier thread or choose a design with a higher stitch count.

If your motif does not appear evenly embossed, your iron surface may not have totally covered the design as you were pressing it. Move your sample to the scrap bag and use it for crazy patching. Or, add beads, lace and charms to the unembossed section to cover it.

Foam

Think the world of embroidery is basically flat? Think again, as foam can add dimension to your work. Foam can be added under embroidery stitching — either all or part of a motif — to raise it to new heights. How high? From 1.5 mm to 4 mm higher than the fabric base.

Criswell Embroidery & Design, Crafty Frames Sampler/Blumenthal Craft Crafter's Images, Recycled Ancestors

The Right Product

Sulky Puffy Foam

Craft foam varies in density and may break apart when used with embroidery motifs, allowing pieces to become lodged in the machine. Sulky of America sells foam designed especially for home embroiderers under the trademark Puffy Foam. Puffy Foam is available in 12 colors and two thicknesses — 2 mm and 3 mm. The product is machine washable and dryable, but will disintegrate with dry cleaning. Puffy Foam is heat sensitive also, so be sure not to touch it with a hot iron.

Raising the Bar

Some embroidery motifs are digitized specifically for use with foam. Those designs offer wide satin stitching to maintain the height of the foam without crushing it. A densely-filled design may as well not have foam under it, as the multiple needle penetrations will flatten the foam structure. Search your favorite design manufacturer for foam-appropriate embroidery designs.

Frequently, foam is used to raise lettering on athletic wear, hats, etc. When using it for this purpose, be sure the lettering is formed with wide satin stitches to get the maximum foam height.

Foam can also be used under appliqués made of other fabrics to give a raised or domed appearance, and it looks great under wide satin-stitch motifs. Layer foam for added roundness in baseballs, tennis balls, etc. To do this, build up extra height in the center, using graduated sizes. Double-check that the built-up areas will fit under your embroidery machine foot — if not, choose a thinner foam or use fewer layers.

Husqvarna Viking, Flower Romance/Sulky of America photo

Use foam to add thickness to a design.

The Right Choices

Keep in mind that the thicker the foam, the higher your design will be raised. This also means that your design will be stiffer. A heavier base fabric is needed to support thicker foam, and more thread will be needed to cover it. Add extra stability to a lightweight fabric by fusing a layer of interfacing to the motif area wrong side before stitching. Because the foam stiffens the motif, select the placement carefully to avoid a standout T-shirt!

When using thicker foams, use a larger size needle and 30-weight thread to cover the foam. The larger size needle will also help prevent breakage from the foam density. Match the foam color to the embroidery thread as closely as possible to prevent show-through.

Stitch it Up

When you make your test sample, check tensions; some machines require a looser tension to avoid compressing the foam.

To use foam under the entire embroidery motif, hoop your work as you normally would using a fabric-appropriate stabilizer. Spray the foam underside with temporary adhesive and position it over the design area. As you embroider the motif, the needle will perforate the foam, which is then torn away after the stitching is complete.

Sulky of America photo

Tip

If any raggedy edges show, use a hair dryer or warm iron to shrink them into the work. Do not touch the foam with the iron; just hover slightly above it and shoot steam.

Some designs will stitch an outline of the motif first, allowing you to pull away the foam once it's anchored around the perimeter. If a design doesn't offer this feature, but it does have an outline to be stitched later, advance to the outline first to perforate the foam and remove the excess before continuing the design from the beginning. Tearing away the foam before covering it with embroidery ensures a smooth edge.

Just A Thought

It's a Frame-Up!

If test stitchouts are piling up in your sewing room, take a trip to your local craft store's framing department and purchase some small frames in a variety of shapes and colors. Mount the embroidery samples in the frames to use as instant gifts, or the basis of a stitchery wall collage.

Sew Man, Snowflakes

42

Home Base

Criswell Embroidery & Design, Coasters with K-Lace Sampler

Foam can also be used as the base for embroidery. Choose open or low-density designs that will not completely perforate the foam, much like the designs used for paper. Running stitch or outline-only designs are ideal.

Rather than hooping the foam, secure water-soluble stabilizer in the hoop and attach the foam to it using temporary spray adhesive or by exposing the stabilizer's adhesive surface. When the embroidery is complete, cut away as much stabilizer as possible, then remove the rest with a damp cloth or sponge.

For a truly unusual foam embroidery technique, look for designs that incorporate a specially digitized outline of very closely spaced needle penetrations. These outlines are intended to be embroidered with an unthreaded needle (see M — Metal on page 64 for more information). The multiple needle penetrations perforate the foam completely, cutting out the embroidered shape so no further finishing is needed!

Just A Thought

My Embroidery Haven, Cutwork 101

Chemical Cutwork

Fiber Etch is a gel formulated to dissolve plant fibers. Used in combination with synthetic thread embroidery on plant fiber fabrics, it's a fast and easy way to create cutwork and other open area designs.

For a different effect, try applying the gel to a blended-fiber cross-dyed fabric, like the velvet shown. Where one fiber is removed, the other is revealed for a dramatic color contrast.

Be sure to follow the manufacturer's instructions and exercise all safety precautions when using Fiber Etch.

Fringe

Fringe is a great way to add dimension to an otherwise flat embroidery motif. A design must be digitized specifically for fringing. There are three designs on the enclosed CD-ROM that are "fringable"— the fringe border, the bookworm and the bookmark.

Enclosed CD-ROM, Bookmark

Enclosed CD-ROM, FringBor

Embroidery designs and instructions for both of these fringe projects can be found on the enclosed CD-ROM.

The Process

During the embroidery process, the area that later becomes fringe is comprised of the extra-long satin stitching. One side (or the center) of those stitches is tacked down with small, dense stitches. If only one side is tacked, the fringe is long and on one side of the stitching only. If the center is tacked down, fringe will form on both sides of the stitching.

After the stitching is complete, carefully remove the bobbin thread and pull the stitches to the project right side to create the fringe. The stitches may be left looped, or they can be cut to create a fuzzy effect. Depending on the type of thread used, brushing may create even fuzzier fringe. Heavier threads create a denser fringe, and those that are more loosely twisted tend to fuzz more than their tightly-twisted counterparts.

The tack-down stitches secure the fringe threads in place while the thread ends create the fringe effect. Depending on the fringe length, small beads may be attached to the thread ends, or the threads may be grouped and/or knotted.

The key to successful fringing is to carefully cut away the bobbin thread only in the areas designed to be fringed. Using a contrasting bobbin thread color makes this process easier, as the bobbin thread is clearly differentiated from the top thread.

Tip

To make the bobbin thread removal process easy, use sharp, pointed scissors and clip carefully. Avoid cutting the top thread if you want looped fringe.

On the Edge

If you plan to sew fringe off the edge of fabric, the process is simple. Off-the-edge fringe can span a finished or unfinished edge, depending on the project and its construction.

1. Hoop water-soluble stabilizer.

2. Make a full-size template of the fringed design and mark the center point on the fabric. Spray the stabilizer with temporary adhesive and adhere the project, aligning the center point with the hoop markings. If you prefer, hoop the project with the stabilizer.

3. Begin to embroider. As you embroider, the fringe stitches will span the fabric edge(s) onto the stabilizer layer only.

4. When the stitching is complete, dissolve the stabilizer to reveal free-standing fringe. Leave looped or cut the loops, depending on the desired look.

Water Ways

Carefully clipping away the bobbin thread from the fringe areas is both tedious and time consuming. Many fringe and tassel motifs are digitized with a color stop before the fringe area (or you can manually stop the machine for this technique).

To make fringing much easier, stop when you get to the fringe area of the embroidery and change the regular bobbin thread to water-soluble thread. Continue stitching through the fringe area, then replace the thread when the fringe area is complete. When the design is totally stitched out, gently swirl it in water to dissolve the thread and release the fringe loops.

Caution: Remember that the water-soluble thread is used only in the fringe area. If you accidentally have it in the machine for prior or subsequent stitching, your entire design will wash away during the dissolution process. The resulting handful of embroidery thread serves as a poignant reminder for next time.

45

Fringe Fury

Embroidery Library, Fringe Peacock

Creative Design, FLO417

Look for fringe loops in the following types of embroidery motifs:
- *Animal fur, manes and tails*
- *Bird feathers*
- *Tassels*
- *Pompoms (think cheerleader)*
- *Dresses and accessories*
- *Collars and cuffs*
- *Flowers*
- *Hair for people and characters*
- *Beards*
- *Toothbrush bristles*
- *Paintbrushes*
- *Bugs*
- *Outlines and lettering*

Fabulous Fringes

Vary the thread weight to give fringe a different look and pay attention to instructions accompanying a design — fringes are digitized for a specific thread weight. Remember, the smaller the number, the heavier the thread weight. The bookworm included on the enclosed CD-ROM is digitized for 40-weight thread, while the fringe bag is made to be stitched in 12-weight thread. Try stitching fringe in variegated thread, Woolly Nylon or metallic for a totally different look.

Laundering will affect the look of the fringe as well. If you have cut fringe and want to preserve the just-stitched look, hand-wash the garment to avoid the thread fraying.

If the fringe tends to curl, lightly steam it to straighten the threads, but don't iron directly on the stitches from the right side.

This bookworm design features variegated 40-weight thread. Find the project instructions and the embroidery design on the enclosed CD-ROM.

Enclosed CD-ROM, Bookworm

Fringing Fabric

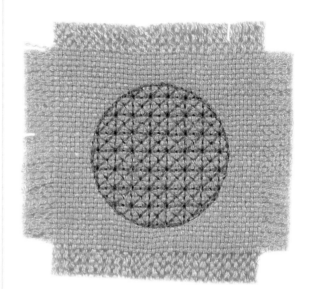

Use embroidery designs as a basis for fringing fabric — fringe inside or outside of the stitching, depending on the look you like, or fringe a shape totally unrelated to the design.

Just A Thought

Pillow Pizzazz

Dig into your pile of test stitch outs and make use of them … no more sewing needed! This clever pre-made pillow (available in several sizes) has a finished "window" for you to just pop in an embroidered stitchout.

Grouping Designs

Essential Elements

To create an oversize embroidery design, you must know the shape and size of each motif before it's stitched. To find out, use full-size templates. Many embroidery designs are packaged with templates, and others have templates available for separate purchase. Each template incorporates a printed image of the motif with lines and dots to indicate the horizontal and vertical axes and the center point.

To make your own templates, turn to your digitizing, customizing or cataloging software. Most programs include an option for printing full-size templates. Be sure to include the centering guides when you print. Templates can be printed on ordinary paper, but transparent templates are easier to use; visit an office supply or art store to purchase transparency film, vellum or tracing paper for printing see-through templates.

If printing is not an option, you can also create your own templates by stitching the design on stabilizer or stabilized fabric. Before removing the template from the hoop, use a permanent marker to transfer the centering guidelines.

Even if your hoop is just 4" square, the size of your embroidery is limited only by your imagination. Combine motifs as building blocks for any size design.

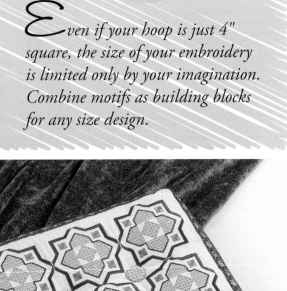

Find the Tile Pillow instructions and embroidery design on the enclosed CD-ROM.

Enclosed CD-ROM, Tile and DecCircl

Tips

- *If possible, stitch only the design outline when creating a template. It will save time and thread.*
- *To shorten the embroidery time when embroidering a large scene, substitute appliqués for large areas of fill stitch or a fabric print for the embroidery background. Some designs are available with special fabric transfers engineered to work with the embroidery motif.*

48

Long Lines

Border hoops are popular machine accessories that allow you to stitch perfectly aligned motifs to create borders in any length you like. Even without a special hoop or software, you can use templates to create continuous borders.

Singer, Card 15

Create long borders, as on the full-length collar of this coat.

Begin by measuring the necessary border length. Compare that to the design measurements and decide whether the motifs should touch, overlap slightly or be separated by a certain amount of space. Also, consider the motif itself. For example, vining motifs may need to overlap slightly for continuity, while densely filled designs that overlap will be lumpy and may create stitching problems.

Draw a guideline for either the design center or its baseline. Extend the guideline along the entire border length. Begin either at one end or the border midpoint. Stitch the first design, then use the template to locate the exact center for the next motif. Rehooping as needed, stitch the next design. Repeat the measuring and stitching until you reach the border's end.

Overall Coverage

Don't let the size of your hoop limit your designs. The only constraints on size are thread, time and patience. With templates and rulers in hand, you can embroider pieces large enough for pillows, quilts and even fabric yardage.

First decide how you will arrange the embroidery motifs. Will they be closely spaced or touching? This arrangement requires the most planning time and the most exacting placement. Will individual motifs be scattered over the project surface? This arrangement doesn't need as much planning because you will need fewer design repeats; unplanned variations in placement may even pass unnoticed. Whenever possible, begin large design arrangements near the center and work outward. This minimizes errors in spacing the individual motifs.

Stabilize the fabric and mark the first design location. Hoop the fabric and stitch. Use a template to locate the next designs in positions around the first motif. Mark their locations. As you embroider, use each motif to double check the accuracy of other placements, then use the fudge factor to make "course corrections" as you go.

To create a scattered arrangement, you could simply arrange templates over the entire fabric surface. A more controlled approach is to draw a grid on the fabric and locate one motif at each intersection.

Use a long quilter's ruler and chalk or removable marker to draw the lines. Begin with a line at a 45-degree angle to the project edge that passes near the project center. Draw parallel lines across the project, then repeat with lines that cross the first set.

Tip

A slanted grid will appear less mechanical and more visually interesting in the finished product than a straight-grain arrangement.

Adjust the gridline spacing to complement the design size, placing the lines closer together for a dense finished arrangement and farther apart for a more open effect. Play with individual designs' rotation for the most varied arrangement.

Historical Embroidery

While the results will never duplicate fine hand needlework completely, digitizers have devised motifs that cleverly mimic a host of historical needlework styles. Some are so close only an expert will know for sure!

Laura's Sewing Studio, Hardangish Squared/2-4-6-8 Pocket Bag Collection

Ayrshire Whitework

Cactus Punch, Ayrshire Baby Bonnet Designs

To duplicate this fine needlework by machine, stitch floral sprays and other simple patterns in white cotton thread on white cotton fabric.

Candlewicking

Designed by Jane, DBJ_CW_01

Traditionally, candlewick designs are composed of repeated French knots that outline a pattern or create a motif. The machine-embroidered version replaces the knots with surprisingly dimensional mounds of stitches for designs with visual and tactile appeal.

Cross Stitch

Machine embroidery can duplicate the rows of Xs with complete accuracy time after time. As an added advantage, there's no counting required, so the designs can be stitched on any fabric (see X — Cross Stitch on page 110 for more information).

Cutwork

Sadia's Designs, Heirloom Lace

Cutwork designs combine traditional stitching with cutout areas and needlewoven bars. The machine embroidery counterpart relies on high-tech stabilizers and digitizing to produce the same appearance.

Crewel Embroidery

OESD, Cutwork & Crewel by Iris Lee, courtesy of Creative Machine Embroidery

The Jacobean patterns and woolly texture of antique crewel embroidery are faithfully reproduced in digitized motifs stitched with wool-blend machine embroidery yarns (see Y — Yarn on page 114 for more information).

Blackwork and Lagartera

Dainty Stitches, Collections 96 and 99, courtesy of Creative Machine Embroidery

Blackwork

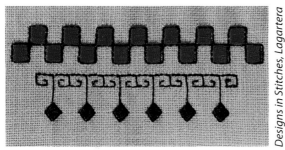

Designs in Stitches, Lagartera Collection, courtesy of Creative Machine Embroidery

Lagartera

Like cross stitch and hardanger, these are traditionally counted techniques. Blackwork is stitched in one color, not necessarily black, with shading and fills created by different stitch patterns. Lagartera is similar, but with small areas of satin fill stitched in red, green or blue.

Redwork

Brother, Card 65

Another one-color technique, Redwork consists of outline-only designs usually stitched in red on a white background. For machine embroidery, look for specially digitized motifs or use only the running stitch outline from a filled and outlined motif.

Hardanger

Laura's Sewing Studio, Hardangish Rainbows, courtesy of Creative Machine Embroidery

Hardanger embroidery is a form of counted thread embroidery that originated in Norway. It's a beautiful, lacy technique based on blocks of stitching alternated with drawn thread areas and needle-made lace. Unlike hardanger stitched by hand, its machine-embroidered counterpart does not have to be stitched on evenweave fabric.

Digitizers use a combination of free-standing lace and cutwork techniques to duplicate hardanger's pulled and reworked threads, or use a wing needle (see O — Out-of-the-Ordinary Needles on page 72 for more information) to create lacy areas within the motif.

Choose cotton or matte-finish embroidery thread for the most authentic appearance, and use a stabilizer that will support blocks of satin stitches when the embroidery is complete.

Molas

Cactus Punch, Mola Style Appliqué

Molas are an indigenous art form of Panama's San Blas Islanders that digitizers have adapted into colorful, playful machine embroidery designs. Best of all, these electronic adaptations eliminate the need for tedious handwork and multiple fabric layers, so the mola motifs can be applied to any apparel and home décor items.

The digitized motifs may include appliquéd pieces, adding authenticity and lowering the stitch count significantly. For an authentic appearance, choose cotton fabrics and embroidery threads in bright, clear colors.

Just A Thought

Stick Up

Use temporary basting sprays in moderation — less is really better. Too much spray adhesive will gum the needle, resulting in skipped stitches and thread breakage. Mechanics warn that it can also drift into the bobbin area and eventually affect machine performance.

Also, most basting sprays are air-soluble, not water-soluble, so washing a project won't remove the sticky residue. In other words, a water-soluble stabilizer sprayed with adhesive will wash away, but the stickiness won't! Even chalk can be trapped and held by basting sprays, resulting in markings that remain until the last of the spray evaporates.

- -

Sticky Situation

When embroidering on unusual materials, adhesive stabilizer holds the oddities in place in the hoop. Choose a stabilizer with a peel-off protective paper, a backing that can be pressed in place with the iron, or one that needs to be dampened to activate the adhesive.

Be sure that your adhesive stabilizer has removal instructions that are compatible with the choice of fabric or embroidable base. For example, a water-soluble stabilizer may not be the best choice for paper, as the water will damage the base.

In-Hoop Sewing

The Basics

Your embroidery hoop can be a sewing tool, too. Made-in-the-hoop projects are usually quick and always accurate, with little or no additional sewing required for completion. They range from super-simple ornaments and coasters to complex teddy bears stitched in pieces and assembled with moveable joints.

Construct made-in-the-hoop items such as coasters and bookmarks in a single layer, usually with a satin stitch edge.

1. Lay water-soluble stabilizer in the embroidery hoop with felt or fabric on top.

2. Stitch the embroidery motif, followed by a running-stitch outline of the project shape.

3. Trim the felt or fabric very close to the outline while the project is still in the hoop.

4. Embroider the satin-stitch edging, covering the running stitches and the fabric raw edges.

5. Dissolve the stabilizer and the project is complete.

By adding an additional layer of fabric behind the embroidery and stabilizer, you can create in-hoop projects with a finished backing. Slide the backing fabric under the hoop before the running-stitch outline and trim both the backing and the face fabric. The satin edging covers the raw edges of both fabrics, and the backing covers the embroidery motif bobbin threads.

Enclosed CD-ROM, Bear

Find the project instructions and embroidery design for this teddy bear on the enclosed CD-ROM.

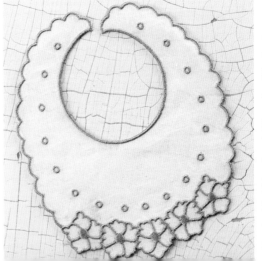

Hatched in Africa, Special Occasion Bibs Set 1, courtesy of Creative Machine Embroidery

Finish Clean

In-hoop projects can also be assembled with a stitch, trim and turn technique.

1. Hoop stabilizer with the face fabric.

2. Stitch the embroidery design or details within the finished project.

3. Lay the backing fabric on the embroidery, right sides together, and sew a running stitch seamline around the project perimeter. The design can be digitized with a gap in the seamline for turning the project, or the digitizer may incorporate another opening within the design.

4. Remove the project from the hoop and trim around the seamline, leaving a narrow seam allowance.

5. Turn the project right-side out, stuff if desired, and close the opening to complete.

Fabulous and Fancy

More complex in-hoop projects incorporate buttonholes, hook-and-loop fasteners and even zippers, all constructed or attached with digitized embroidery. Decorative stitch patterns conceal raw edges, and even curves or complicated shapes are stitched perfectly every time.

The accuracy and consistency of in-hoop sewing can be used to great advantage when sewing doll clothes or small stuffed animals. Rather than cutting small pieces and struggling to keep the seamlines accurate around tight curves and corners, stitch layers of fabric together in the hoop to make individual pieces, then assemble them.

Tips

- *Always follow the digitizer's instructions for an in-hoop project. Most include detailed, step-by-step instructions, often with pictures. Remember that the reason for a particular step may not be apparent until later in the process, and the digitizer has determined the best order for the project steps.*
- *Many in-hoop projects call for spray adhesive. Use it sparingly, or substitute tape or pins placed outside the stitching area.*
- *Choose firmly woven fabrics for satin-edge projects, since loose weaves or fabrics with heavy yarns may ravel or pull free of the stitching.*
- *Trim-and-turn projects can be made from knit fabrics, too. Be aware that the fabric stretch may affect the finished shape, and experiment with vertical and horizontal stretch or a combination of the two.*
- *If the project calls for stuffing, polyester fiberfill is a good choice. Insert tiny bits of stuffing and pack them firmly into the nooks and crannies of the shape. For a soft, squeezable fabric toy, use polyester stuffing clusters that retain their loft inside the shape.*

Jewelry

*N*ecklaces, bracelets, earrings, watches — you can create an entire wardrobe of unique gems with machine embroidery. Stitch pieces in colors that coordinate with a favorite outfit, or go for glitz with metallic threads and added beads. The techniques range from complex to utterly simple, so there's something for everyone.

Use the design and follow the instructions on the enclosed CD-ROM to make your own jewelry pieces.

Findings First

Begin your jewelry making with a trip to the jewelry and bead department at your favorite craft or discount store. There, you'll discover the findings, or special jewelry components, needed for finishing your embroidered accessories. Findings include earring wires, pin backs, watch faces, jump rings, clasps and chains. They are available in gold, silver and copper finishes. Inexpensive plated metal versions are readily available for costume jewelry pieces, while true gold and silver findings can be purchased for heirloom projects.

Invest in a pair of jewelry pliers to make manipulating the tiny findings easier. Wire cutters and other tools of the trade are handy when you're ready to make a bigger investment.

Sudberry House, Sew Magic and Sewing Watch Kit, courtesy of Sew News

Bead Different Embroidery, Jewelry and Embellishments

Some findings for embroidered jewelry are a bit more unusual. Cardboard makes a handy base for pendants; look for sturdy mat or illustration board with the store's art supplies. Button forms, especially the largest size, can also be used to mount embroidered jewelry. Rattail and other cords and ribbons from the notions department can be used in place of chain, and humble embroidery floss is perfect for twisting your own cord in any of several hundred colors.

Maybe the most unusual jewelry finding of all — foam hair rollers — is available in the health and beauty aisle, or even at the local discount store. They form the base for embroidered beads perfect in necklaces, key chains, cell phone dangles and scissors fobs. Simply stitch a band of embroidery, sew it into a tube and gather it around a section of foam roller to make a bead with a central hole, ready to string.

Embroidered jewelry can be accented with beads and metal charms to add sparkle. These findings also add a bit of weight to embroidered pendants and pins, which can improve the way the jewelry hangs when worn.

Tip

Here's an unusual way to add weight while commemorating the date the embroidered jewel was made: Tuck a coin with the appropriate date inside as the piece is being finished!

Fabric Flair

When making fabric jewelry, look for medium-weight materials light enough to finish smoothly, but heavy enough to avoid transparency. If you are making an outfit, consider using a scrap of the fabric or coordinating lining material as the base for a unique matching pendant or pin. If the fabric alone is too thin or hard to handle, back it with a lightweight fusible interfacing before embroidering and constructing the jewelry.

Another way to coordinate jewelry with a particular apparel item is to match the thread to the fabric color. This is a great way to accent purchased clothing when fabric scraps are not available.

Criswell Embroidery & Design, Crafty Frames Sampler/ Blumenthal Crafts Crafter's Images, Recycled Ancestors

The same technique applied to shrinkable plastic yields tiny frames that can be mounted on ribbon or hung on chain to make commemorative photo jewelry. It's a modern spin on the traditional portrait locket!

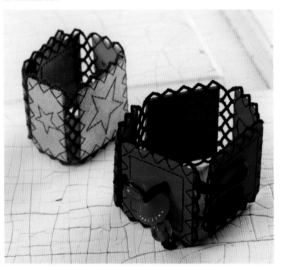

Criswell Embroidery & Design, Bracelets with K-Lace Sampler

Don't forget non-traditional fabrics like ribbon, too. An embroidered ribbon needs only a clasp to become a choker necklace or bracelet (see N — Narrow Stuff on page 70 for more information).

For a really unusual spin on embroidered jewelry, press ordinary foam (like Puffy Foam) to shrink and firm its texture, then stitch with special embroidery designs that use no thread. Instead, the needle penetrations perforate the foam to create cutout shapes that can be linked with ribbon, cord, or even embroidered lace to make cuff bracelets and more.

Lovely Lace

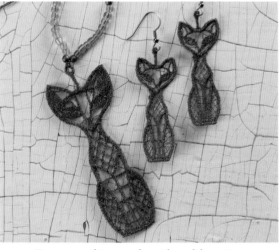

Criswell Embroidery & Design, Kae's Cats K-Lace Sampler, courtesy of Sew News

Free-standing embroidered lace is a great jewelry-making technique. Its texture is similar to metal filigree, and the open areas between stitches provide natural holes for adding jump rings or other findings. Look for tiny charm bracelet motifs, matching designs for earring and pendant sets, and even embroidered chains for mounting the charms of thread.

For the simplest lace jewelry, stitch the motifs on water-soluble stabilizer and dissolve the stabilizer. Slip an earring wire or jump ring

through a hole at the top of the motif (many include embroidered rings just for that purpose) or mount the motif on a chain or cord, and the jewelry is ready to wear. If the finished lace motifs curl, press them with a steam iron to flatten. Add a bit of spray starch or fabric stiffener if needed.

Sparkle Plenty

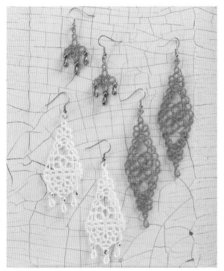

Criswell Embroidery & Design, Chandelier Jewelry K-Lace Sampler, courtesy of Sew News

Jewelry, of course, is meant to have some flash. Add beads and crystals to stitched lace or other motifs to add glitz. Stitch the beads in place with matching thread and a fine needle, or even string them from the jewelry as a tassel or fringe. Glue crystals in place with clear craft adhesive, or apply iron-on or heat-set crystals with a special tool.

Don't overlook the possibilities of stitching with metallic thread. Machine embroidery metallics are available in many colors, even in multiple versions of silver and gold. Be sure to look for a smooth, consistent finish and round profile that make the thread more appropriate for the rigors of machine embroidery.

Use metallic thread for an entire motif or simply to accent a design stitched in other threads. For example, use metallic gold as the outline color in place of black embroidery thread. Good quality metallic machine embroidery threads can even be used in the bobbin for stitching metallic lace jewelry motifs.

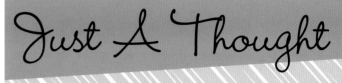

Just A Thought

Quilt Labels

Enclosed CD-ROM, BookCov3

Machine embroidery is a great medium for creating labels for quilts and other crafts. Stitch an embroidered frame and fill it with embroidered lettering that details important facts about the work. To include more information or smaller lettering, use permanent fabric pens to hand write the details within the embroidered frame.

If you don't trust your own handwriting, use a word processing program to print the label information, then trace the words onto the fabric label. Or, print the words directly onto the fabric, then embroider a frame or accent design around them.

At minimum, the label should give the maker's name and the year the project was completed. You might also choose to include the recipient's name, the city where the work was done, details about the project's materials and construction, or a title for the work.

Kaleidoscope
Designing by Degrees

If you have ever played with one of these fascinating toys, you'll remember the riot of color and never-ending variety of patterns it produced. Use the rotation functions of your embroidery machine or software to create kaleidoscopic patterns of your own from embroidery motifs and thread.

To design repeating patterns, begin with a bit of simple math. There are 360 degrees in a circle; divide 360 by the number of designs in your kaleidoscope and you'll know how much rotation is needed for each one.

For a six-repeat kaleidoscope, use the formula from the paragraph above: 360 ÷ 6 = 60. This means that there are 60 degrees of difference between design centers. Therefore, use motifs with 0, 60, 120, 180, 240 and 300 degrees of rotation. For an eight-repeat design, you would use this formula: 360 ÷ 8 = 45. This means that the difference is 45 degrees: 0, 45, 90, 135, 180, 225, 270 and 315.

Brother, Card 28

The eight designs in this kaleidoscope are rotated by 45 degrees.

Once you have rotated the designs, position them next to each other so their sides almost touch, creating a ring of embroidery. Larger motifs will need to be placed farther from the kaleidoscope's center to avoid overlaps, so larger motifs will make a larger overall design.

Brother, Card 28

The six designs in this kaleidoscope are rotated by 60 degrees.

Time to Reflect

Enclosed CD-ROM, CatFish

Observe the negative space in these examples to see how mirror imaging adds interest to the kaleidoscope.

For a truly kaleidoscopic arrangement, add mirror imaging to the technique. Use the mirroring command to flip every other motif, then reposition the designs if necessary. Mirror imaging works only with asymmetric motifs, so choose designs that are not the same on all sides. If a motif is symmetric to the left and right, try mirroring it top to bottom to produce the variety needed for a successful kaleidoscope.

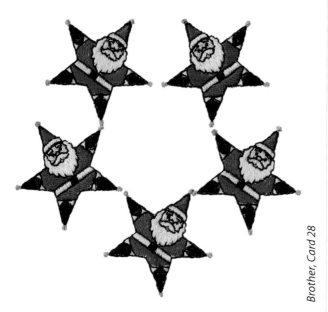

Brother, Card 28

Some motifs may combine more gracefully without the mechanics of mathematical rotation. To make this kaleidoscopic ring, turn the stars with the free-rotation tools and position them so their points just touch.

Wordplay

EmbroideryArts, Celtic Alphabet

EmbroideryArts, Arabesque 4 Alphabet

Normally used in twos or threes for traditional monograms, decorative letters can also be used as elements in lacy kaleidoscopic designs. Play with rotation and mirroring, and even allow the letter flourishes to overlap. Create a design from a friend's initial or write a secret message in the design's embroidered swirls.

Another Thought

Buy photo editing software that automatically creates kaleidoscopic arrangements from any photograph or computer graphic file. Use this software

A Bit of Stitch, Classic Frames

to print a kaleidoscope on fabric, then use the fabric as an appliqué motif or background for embroidery. Why not scan an embroidered design, make a kaleidoscopic print of it, and use the printed fabric to frame the embroidered motif? The possibilities are endless! *Note:* Some designs can legally be used *only* for embroidery.

Lace

On the list of unusual embroidery techniques, stitching on nothing at all ranks high. That's the essence of free-standing lace embroidery.

Technically, free-standing motifs are stitched on water-soluble stabilizer. Digitizers create a self-supporting structure of understitching that carries the finished designs when the stabilizer is dissolved, leaving only soft and airy lace.

Criswell Embroidery & Design, Spring Décor K-Lace Sampler

Thread Tales

In the absence of fabric, thread becomes the all-important ingredient for stitching lace. Thread size is critical, so be sure to follow the digitizer's guidelines. Fine cotton thread creates the softest lace, making it ideal for drapable apparel trims. Rayon threads give laces the appearance of silk. Natural silk thread can be used for embroidered lace, too, for a luxuriously supple finished product.

Fabric That's Nothing

Free-standing lace motifs have high stitch counts, so the stabilizer needs to be sturdy. Two types work well: plastic film water-soluble stabilizers and mesh-type water soluble stabilizers.

Plastic film water-soluble stabilizers are available in different weights; choose the heaviest weight for lace motifs, or combine two or more layers of lighter weight stabilizer in the hoop. Mesh-type water-soluble stabilizers are less prone to tearing, making them ideal for free-standing lace. Use one or two layers to support lace stitches.

Hoop the stabilizer tightly in the smallest hoop that will hold the design. This will counteract the distortion created by the lace motifs' high stitch count. The lace structure depends on exact alignment of finishing stitches over the understitching. Use hooping aids, if available, to hold the thin stabilizer firmly in the hoop.

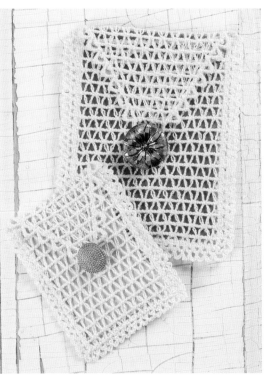

Cindy Losekamp, Crocheted Crudités

These faux-crochet bags were stitched with cotton thread.

Polyester embroidery threads are a popular choice for embroidered lace. They tend to be stiffer than cotton laces, which can be a drawback for apparel applications. But polyester's extra body and wide range of colors makes it a good choice for free-standing lace projects such as flowers, ornaments and bowls. For something truly different, experiment with metallic threads for free-standing laces. For more on this idea, see J — Jewelry on page 56.

For more on this idea, see J — Jewelry on page 56.

Tip

Be sure to remove all of the stabilizer residue for the softest finished lace. Use a combination of rinsing and soaking the finished embroidery for the best results. Check the manufacturer's instructions for specifics such as water temperature.

Make Something of It

To assemble lace pieces with a sewing machine, trim away the excess stabilizer close to the embroidery. Abut the edges to be joined, and connect them with a zigzag stitch that swings back and forth between the pieces. Use matching thread in needle and bobbin for a virtually invisible join.

To assemble lace pieces by hand, remove all of the stabilizer first to soften the lace. Thread a thin needle with matching thread, and assemble the sections by whipstitching the edges together.

To attach embroidered lace to fabric, stitch the lace header to the fabric using your sewing machine. For an embellished finish, attach the lace and add decorative machine stitches or wing needle work close to the lace edge.

Fun on Fabric

Lace motifs aren't always free-standing — that is, the kind of design that supports itself after the stabilizer is removed. Some lace motifs are digitized to be stitched the traditional way — on fabric.

To stitch faux lace trim on fabric, select a contrasting thread color so the embroidery stands out. Use white on black for a stunning combination, or pastels for a baby or springtime theme. Metallic threads add sparkle to otherwise flat embroidery.

Lacy motifs and small embroideries can also be used to create heirloom trims reminiscent of fine Swiss edgings and insertions. Choose lightweight cotton thread (60- or 80-weight) and stitch the design on matching color cotton batiste. Trim insertions parallel to the embroidered motifs and seam them into the garment to finish their raw edges.

To make an edging, stitch a satin scallop alongside the embroidered motifs and trim away the excess fabric close to the scalloped edge. Apply a thin coat of seam sealant on the scallop's wrong side to seal the edging for durability during washing and wear.

Criswell Embroidery & Design, *More Baskets of K-Lace*

Digitizers have discovered the flexibility of lace shapes in creating dimensional projects. Most often, a project is stitched in pieces, then the pieces are laced or sewn together.

Metal

Stitching on metal is something many people shy away from, thinking it will harm the sewing machine, or worse yet, harm them personally with flying shrapnel. But neither of those is the case, if you follow some simple steps to success. You can create the look of folkloric tin punching with much less work than doing it with punches and other handworking tools.

The Right Stuff

Several options exist for stitchable metals (none of which will recommend sewing with them on the packaging) so use your instincts for what will work.

Craft or Tooling Foil

Craft foil is a flexible metal that is sold by the roll or the sheet. It is available in silver (aluminum), brass and copper finishes. Some manufacturers make thinner versions in colors as well. Designed for use with traditional tooling techniques, craft foil is available in several weights, known as gauges, and several widths or by the sheet. The larger the gauge number, the thinner the metal. Check the metal's gauge (thickness); 36- or 38-gauge metal works well for embroidery stitching and is .005" and .004" thick, respectively. Craft foil is soft and pliable, and it works well for large projects where excess metal extends beyond the hoop size.

Embroidered craft foil makes the perfect lampshade covering. Use the design and follow the instructions on the enclosed CD-ROM to make your own.

Enclosed CD-ROM, MetalSW

Enclosed CD-ROM, MetBord

Enclosed CD-ROM, MetBord, FBordCor

This metal box insert and napkin ring are the perfect projects for trying metalwork. Use the design and follow the instructions on the enclosed CD-ROM to make your own box insert or napkin ring.

Flashing

Another metal option is flashing, which is available in home improvement stores. Intended for roofing, this metal comes on a roll in silver or copper finishes. It's generally less flexible than craft foil, making it fine for small, hoop-size projects, but a bit more difficult to work with on larger projects that overlap the hoop size.

Enclosed CD-ROM, MetStars

This star garland uses metal flashing. Use the design and follow the instructions on the CD-ROM to make your own garland.

Rustable Metals

For a country look, pre-rusted or ready-to-rust steel is available in multiple weights in both sheets and rolls. Ready-to-rust metal transforms itself when spritzed with apple cider vinegar or a combination of bleach and cider vinegar.

To maintain the color and finish, spray with a light coat of clear protectant after your embroidery is finished.

Mesh

Several companies sell metal mesh, a very fine screening, which holds embroidered needle holes well. Look for it with the tooling foil in brass and copper finishes.

Enclosed CD-ROM, MetBord and MBordCor

Metal mesh is the perfect accessory for a candle. This wrap allows the candlelight to glow through the punched holes. Use the design and follow the instructions on the enclosed CD-ROM to make your own candle wrap.

Other Tools

In addition to metal, you will need a number of other tools to make embroidering on metal a successful experience.

~*Adhesive or water-activated adhesive stabilizer:* A firm hold is necessary to avoid design distortion, and these types of stabilizers will help hold the metal in place for the embroidery process.

~*Decorative punches:* These tools, typically used for scrapbooking, will also punch lightweight metals. These decorative holes are perfect for hanging or design accents.

~*Felt:* Assemble scraps of felt slightly larger than the embroidery hoop. Without a protective layer of felt or fleece under your work, the rough metal edges left from the needle (the "cheese grater effect") will scar the machine bed.

Fiskars Decorative Punches

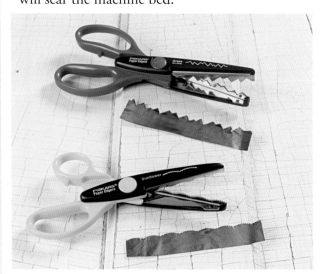

Fiskars Decorative-Edge Scissors

- *Large hand-sewing needle:* If you're making an ornament or something else that will hang, a large hand-sewing needle can be used to thread a hanger through the finished piece.
- *Masking tape:* This notion helps to secure edges that may try to curl up, especially on metal flashing.
- *Nail or awl:* Use these instead of punches to create hanging holes in metalwork.
- *Pair of old scissors or tin snips:* Avoid the temptation to use your good dress-making shears for this purpose! You can also use decorative-edge scissors to finish the edges of stitched pieces — use a dedicated pair for metal, as the metal quickly dulls the scrapbook variety scissors.
- *Size 100 or larger sewing machine needle:* Most home embroidery machines will take up to a size 120 needle, sometimes requiring special ordering from your machine dealer. The needle doesn't have to be new, as it's simply puncturing the metal, so keep old needles on hand for metal embroidery.
- *Small hammer and old mouse pad:* These two items work together to create a hammered finish on your metalwork.

Machine Settings

Insert a large needle into the machine, keeping in mind that the larger the needle, the larger the hole left in the metal. Even though no thread is used for this metalwork, you may need to thread the machine both top and bottom to outsmart the machine's threading sensors. Some machines will stop or beep to warn of a low bobbin or a broken top thread, so sewing totally without thread may not be an option.

If your machine has thread sensors, place a full bobbin in the machine. On the top, thread the machine through the last thread guide before the needle. Instead of actually threading the needle, tape the thread end to the side of the machine. This makes the machine think that it has thread, but in reality, it's not stitching with any.

Some machines allow you to control the stitching speed. If this feature is available, slow the speed for metalwork.

Selecting Designs

Look for designs with minimal needle penetrations. The ideal embroidery motif has only single lines of stitching forming the pattern.

On the enclosed CD-ROM, the star, border and Southwest motifs offer versions digitized specifically for metalwork. The star has several parts which can be used separately or together and includes an optional border.

When selecting commercially digitized designs from other sources, look for outline-only motifs, such as Redwork or the outline portion of appliqué motifs. Most appliqué designs stitch a placement line as the first pass on the embroidery process, and this line of stitching is all that's needed for metalwork. Fill designs may also work; some fill designs have a running stitch outline (usually sewn last) and this is the only design portion needed for metalwork. Skip over other portions of the design to get to the outline.

Avoid designs with dense fill patterns and multiple stitching in the same hole, as these may enlarge the metal hole and damage the design integrity. If you really want to use a design with multiple penetrations, use a smaller needle to avoid damage, but be aware that the machine may not always hit the same hole exactly and metal piercings are permanent.

Use your embroidery software or on-screen editing to enlarge an embroidery motif to space out the needle penetrations and avoid weakening the metal.

Hooping

Depending on the flexibility of the metal, it's easiest to work with small projects that fit within the confines of the embroidery hoop. Managing oversized and/or stiff metal can be tricky, but with the help of masking tape, it can be done.

1. Cut the metal slightly larger than the size needed for your project, as it can be trimmed after stitching/piercing.

2. Select a hoop size larger than the metal project if possible (most embroidery machines offer a choice of hoop sizes).

3. Firmly secure adhesive stabilizer in the hoop.

4. Spray the *underside* of the stabilizer with temporary adhesive, and secure the felt to prevent damage to the machine from the pierced hole rough edges.

5. Depending on the resiliency of the metal, substitute tear-away or cut-away stabilizer and spray it with temporary adhesive to hold the metal in place. Remember that there is no thread used with the stitches, so either type of stabilizer will simply pull away from the metal underside. For better adhesion, use pins diagonally across the corners to hold the metal in place.

6. Activate the adhesive stabilizer either by moistening or by peeling away the protective paper.

7. Center the metal in the hoop. If necessary, tape the metal edges to the stabilizer and/or hoop. Any movement during the embroidery process will cause design distortion and potential machine damage.

Making Holes

As with any embroidery, test-stitch before sewing the real project. Stitch on a piece of metal so that you have a feel for the process, are comfortable with the noise and can check for any errant stitches you may want to skip over when stitching the actual project.

1. Some machines begin the embroidery process with a centering stitch. When working with metal, manually skip over this stitch to avoid a permanent hole in the project center. *Note:* Many machines return to the center point at the end of the embroidery pattern as well, so stop the machine prior to that jump.

2. Hold the metal firmly against the stabilizer as you stitch. Because of its rigidity, it has a tendency to ride up on the needle. Keeping the metal firmly against the machine will cut down on the noise as well.

3. If your machine or embroidery motif offers a perimeter basting/outline function, use it to add a border to the motif you're piercing, or pierce a border using the conventional machine straight stitch.

4. After the embroidery is complete, remove the stabilizer, following the manufacturer's instructions. Recycle the felt for another metal project. *Note:* You can reuse the adhesive stabilizer for more metalwork as long as it remains sticky and isn't torn.

Beyond the Basics

If your metal embroidery is going to be an ornament, leave a border around it and add an extension to the top as you trim off the excess. You can punch the extension to place hanging ribbon or thread. To make a hole, use a nail, awl or decorative punch.

To accent a pierced border, thread heavy thread through it like a child's sewing card. Work with short lengths of thread, as each time thread is pulled through the holes the sharp edges will wear on it.

Enclosed CD-ROM, MetStars

Thread yarn or floss through the pierced border.

Your metalwork can be used many ways. Frame it like you would with a photo, or add it to pre-finished items like wooden boxes or papier-mâché shapes. You can also use metal shapes as gift tags if the sharp underside is covered with felt or paper for protection. Lampshades are another great use for embroidered metal.

Caution!

The underside and edges of metalwork are very sharp and care is needed when handling. Never expose the underside of the embroidery, as the "cheese grater effect" will damage anything it touches, including people.

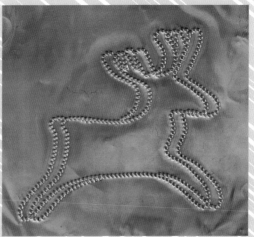

Husqvarna Viking, Appliqué

If one needle is good, multiples might be more interesting! Twin- or triple-needles can be used for metalwork, increasing the number of holes that outline the design.

Tip

Hole-y cow! If you have errant needle holes, or adjacent holes in the design appear to meld into one, use a small, flat screwdriver and push the hole flanges closed from the metal underside. It's not a perfect solution, but will help camouflage the mistake.

Narrow Stuff

Enclosed CD-ROM, DogCollr and CatCollr

Embroidering on narrow things like ribbon, braid, trim, webbings, etc. can be a challenge. Common sense tells us that it's easier to embroider on something wide, then trim it to narrow, but that's not always possible; ribbons and narrow trims have pre-finished edges and must be embroidered as they come off the reel or spool.

Positioning is key whenever trimming or repositioning later isn't an option. In some instances, like our pet collar projects on the enclosed CD-ROM, the width of your embroidery target is only ¾" to 1", and centering the design is critical.

Use the designs and follow the instructions on the enclosed CD-ROM to create a collar and a dog treat jar for your favorite pet.

Planning Ahead

If you're embroidering several repeats of a motif along the narrow length, combine them in embroidery software or on the machine's touch-screen until they reach the maximum length of the hoop. This will mean fewer repositionings and less chance for error with repeated groupings.

Enclosed CD-ROM, DogBone

Holding On

The secret to narrow embroidery is adhesive stabilizer. Whether you choose one with a protective paper covering or one that is moisture-activated depends on the fiber content and characteristics of the embroidery base. If you want to embroider on silk ribbon, for example, water is not an ingredient you want to add to the mix, for fear of spotting. Therefore, use an adhesive stabilizer with the protective paper covering.

You can also create an adhesive stabilizer by choosing your favorite tear-away stabilizer and pairing it with temporary spray adhesive.

Since most narrow things will have both sides showing once the embroidery is complete, removing all of the stabilizer is important so it doesn't look ugly on the underside of a carefully tied ribbon, or on the back side of a personalized dog leash. Use water-soluble adhesive stabilizer in these situations.

Sudberry House, Fun Fish/Flip-Flop Watch Kit

Cover-Ups

Sometimes narrow things don't have a smooth surface — like nylon webbing used for pet collars and leashes, or velvet ribbon. Use a permanent vinyl topper such as Dry Cover-Up to help the embroidery stitches stay on top of the uneven surface.

Hoop It Up

It's best not to hoop narrow things, but rather to adhere them to adhesive stabilizer.

Husqvarna Viking, Geometric Sensation

1. Hoop the stabilizer and score the protective paper on the adhesive stabilizer slightly wider than the embroidery base, and peel it away (or moisten a narrow width of the hooped stabilizer for moisture-activated varieties).

2. In most instances, you will be stitching multiple design repeats along the length of the base, so carefully mark the center points and repeats of the motif using pins or a removable marker. Position the narrow item on the stabilizer accordingly.

3. Spray the topper with temporary adhesive and adhere it to the surface of the embroidery base. Use the needle tracing feature on your machine to check the design placement and to be sure the narrow item is straight in the hoop — if it wavers, the design will not be even from the edges along the length. *Note:* The topper is another layer that goes over the narrow item to help keep the stitches on top of the perhaps uneven surface.

4. Once all the embroidery is complete, clip the jump threads and remove the stabilizer(s), following the manufacturer's instructions. Press the narrow item from the wrong side.

Out-of-the-Ordinary Needles

Using double, triple or wing needles to stitch embroidery motifs can add interesting effects. This also requires caution, unless the design is specifically digitized for that purpose.

Rebecca Says

- *Some machines may move multiple threads more smoothly if the thread winds off the spools in opposite directions.*
- *Remember **not** to use the automatic needle threader with multiple needles!*
- *Some manufacturers recommend against using the automatic thread cutter, too, so disable that function before embroidering with multiple needles.*

Multiple Needles

Most embroidery machines can accommodate multiple needles — usually two or three needles attached to a single shank and inserted into the machine as a single needle would be. Be sure to check your machine's instruction book for information on threading multiple needles — generally both threads follow the same threading pattern until they reach the needles, though they may be separated at the tension discs, depending on the machine's configuration.

A variety of types of double or twin needles are available. Look for them in sizes 70 to 100 and in universal, stretch, embroidery, denim and metallic designations. A double hemstitch needle is also available with one regular needle and one wing needle on a single shaft, but these aren't recommended for embroidery stitching, except perhaps for outline motifs on metal, where a larger hole is desired for threading yarn or floss.

Double needles have two number designations on the package. The first is the spacing between the needles, listed in millimeters (1.6 to 8.0), and the second number is the needle size. A designation of 1.6/70 indicates 1.6 mm between the tips of two size 70 needles.

  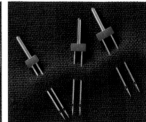

Design Options

It's not a good idea to stitch filled embroidery motifs with multiple needles, as the thread density multiplies and the stitching becomes visually distorted. Ultimately, the needle set will break, and multiple needles cost more to replace than single needles.

Instead, look for outline motifs to try with multiple needles — they have much lower stitch counts than filled or patterned designs and can look quite interesting. Another good choice is the first stitching line on appliqué designs.

Keep in mind that the stitched design will have clearly defined parallel stitching lines when the embroidery machine arm is moving forward and backward. The needle spacing will determine the space between the lines.

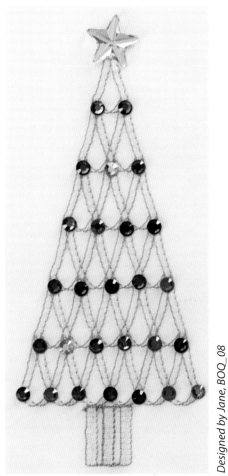

Designed by Jane, BOQ_08

Add iron-on accents to double-needle designs.

Thread Choices

One bobbin picks up stitches from the multiple upper needles, so if you look carefully at the needles, one is generally just a bit shorter than the other to allow for this sharing in the stitch formation process.

Most metallics work well with multiple needles and the combination of gold and silver creates an elegant look for outline designs.

Try using different kinds of threads together in double needles — perhaps a 30-weight in one needle and a 40-weight in the other, or a cotton thread in one and rayon in the other. There's plenty of opportunity for needle play! Remember, it never hurts to experiment if you follow basic embroidery principles.

Husqvarna Viking, Designer 1 Sampler

When using multiple needles, they can be threaded with the same or different thread colors, depending on the desired effect. Choosing closely related thread colors results in almost a shadowed effect, while high-contrast picks create more defined lines.

Down Under

In addition to mixing threads between needles, try using a darker bobbin thread when sewing on lightweight or sheer fabrics. The darker thread will give a shadowed look to the stitching and actually create a muted fabric tone when used with widely spaced needles.

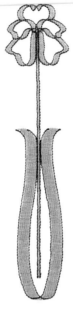

Designed by Jane, BOQ_08

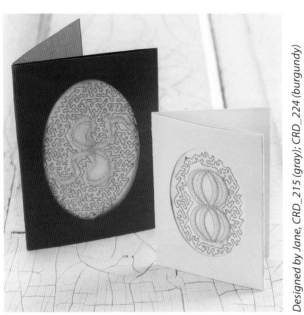

Designed by Jane, CRD_215 (gray); CRD_224 (burgundy)

Tension Headaches

Because a single bobbin is servicing multiple needles, you may need to fine-tune the tension adjustments to produce a flat motif. Double and triple needles tend to tunnel or make a raised area between needles as the bobbin creates a zigzag to grab multiple upper threads. Some motifs look great with the added dimension and others don't, so adjust the tension according to your preference, design selection and fabric.

Threading Bliss

Klaer International Needle Threader

Threading multiple needles can be tricky since the automatic threading mechanisms don't work with more than one needle. Use a needle threader to make the task easier.

Wing Needles

Hand embroiderers know that many beautiful patterns can be created by systematically increasing the tension on stitches to pull groups of fabric yarns together. To mimic this pulled thread technique with an embroidery machine, a savvy stitcher looks to an oddly-shaped notion called a wing needle.

The wing needle gets its name from the two broad appendages that flank the needle shaft. This broad profile opens a hole in the fabric by pushing the fibers apart, and the stitches keep the hole open by exerting tension in opposing directions. It's really easier than it sounds!

Use the design and follow the instructions on the enclosed CD-ROM to make your own embroidered linen towel using wing needle work.

Needle Know-How

Wing needles are available in three sizes: 90/14, 100/16 and 120/18. Since the needle should push the fabric apart rather than breaking its yarns while opening holes, choose a needle size appropriate for the fabric type. The size 100/16 needle usually produces good results.

For fine or delicate fabrics, select the smallest wing needle. Or, for an even gentler alternative, use a regular needle (without wings) in size 100/16 to open the holes.

If your machine has a straight-stitch plate, with a hole rather than a slot for the needle, be sure to replace it with the zigzag throat plate before using a wing needle.

Threads and Fabrics

Traditionally, wing needle work is done with a cotton thread that matches the fabric color to emphasize the pattern of holes rather than the stitches. Threads used in wing needle work must have a fine diameter so the

repeated stitches into each hole do not fill the hole with thread. Choose a 60- or 80-weight heirloom cotton thread, or substitute 40-weight or smaller embroidery thread.

Use regular machine embroidery bobbin thread if the wrong side will not show, or wind the bobbin with the same thread used in the needle.

Choose a natural fiber fabric that will not relax into its original flat state after stitching. Some fabric blends can also be used. Work with light- to medium-weight fabrics that are not too tightly woven.

Simply Stable

The best stabilizer for wing-needle work is none at all, since the design should be able to move the fabric yarns around to make the holes. But practically speaking, some stabilization is necessary.

Apply two or more coats of spray starch or liquid fabric stabilizer to the material. Press with a warm iron between coats. The ideal result is a firm, paper-like texture. Hoop the stabilized fabric and proceed with the wing-needle embroidery.

Once the wing-needle portion of the motif is finished, add a layer of tear-away stabilizer under the hooped fabric to provide support for the rest of the embroidery stitches.

Paper

Paper is really a loose term that applies to a host of different materials, from lightweight cardboard to fragile tissue. In between are many papers with high fiber content and enough durability to support stitching, including machine embroidered designs.

Paper Perfection

The easiest papers to embroider are those with a high rag (fiber) content. This doesn't necessarily mean the paper is made from rags, though some recycled papers may be! These papers look and feel much like non-woven stabilizers, and can support lots of stitches.

Art and scrapbooking papers with high rag content are often labeled "handmade," even though a machine may have done much of the production work. They are characterized by lots of texture, with thick and thin areas and uneven colors. Some are almost as soft as fabric.

Cross-stitch motifs stitch beautifully on paper.

Cardstock, a popular paper among scrapbookers and paper artists, can also be used for embroidered motifs such as outline-only

Find the embroidery designs and project instructions for the Handmade Book and Photo Mat on the enclosed CD-ROM.

quilting motifs and Redwork designs. Cardstock is stiff and more brittle than fibrous papers, so it perforates and tears more easily, something to keep in mind as you choose designs to embroider.

Crisp, brittle papers like vellum and thin, flimsy ones like tissue may be adapted for embroidery with the addition of stabilizer. Since the stabilizer will significantly change the paper's appearance, these lightweight papers are better suited for use as a base to which embroidered paper is attached or as small add-on elements in a larger layout.

My Fair Lady Designs, Paper Stipple

My Fair Lady Designs, Wedding Stipple Set 1

Embroidered paper is an ideal ingredient for cardmaking.

Design Decisions

Some design categories that work especially well on paper are: openwork, quilting, appliqué designs with non-satin stitch edgings, Redwork and chain-stitch designs. Some digitizers are even creating collections especially for paper embroidery! Try to avoid very densely filled designs and motifs with lots of understitching or columns of consistent-width satin stitches that will perforate and split the paper. To adapt an otherwise unsuitable design for paper embroidery, try one of these techniques:

- Delete the understitching to reduce the number of needle penetrations.
- Stitch only the understitching — it may not form a pleasing design, but you might be surprised with a lacy, abstract motif!

- Reduce the stitch density in customizing software.
- Enlarge the design at the machine or in software without increasing the stitch count — this is another way to lower the design's density.

Tip

If your embroidery format begins each design with a centering stitch, manually skip over this stitch to avoid an unwanted hole in the paper. Some machines also return to the center point at the end of the embroidery pattern, so stop the machine prior to that jump.

Suitable Stabilizers

Stabilizer is essential for successful embroidery on paper. Both permanent and removable stabilizers can be used, but keep the removal method in mind if you choose a non-permanent stabilizer. Most papers are not water-friendly, so wash-away stabilizers are inappropriate, and tear-aways should be removed with caution so the paper does not tear as well.

Since most paper is not hooped for embroidery — avoiding the risks of hoop burns and tears — adhesive stabilizers are ideal. Adhesive tear-away stabilizer is great for most paper embroidery. Simply hoop the stabilizer and expose the adhesive surface. Attach the paper and embroider. When the stitching is complete, lift the paper edges away from the stabilizer and trim away the excess stabilizer. Even though it's a tear-away, trimming with scissors relieves stress on the paper around the embroidery edges.

Use adhesive cut-aways for opaque papers, where there is confidence that the stabilizer will not shadow through the paper. For transparent papers, use clear stabilizer for a no-show finish, especially if the embroidery is an open motif.

Nice Notions

Use regular embroidery or sewing needles for stitching on paper. Smaller needle sizes (70/10 to 75/11) are preferable, since the needle holes are permanent and larger needles leave larger holes.

Most threads work well for paper embroidery, but save heavy or coarse threads for surface work (couching) or bobbin embroidery, so they do not drag through the paper to create large holes or tears.

For cutting and trimming paper, set aside a special pair of scissors just for paper crafts. Rotary cutters and craft knives are also handy, and the variety of punches, decorative scissors and eyelet setters for paper crafting can be used for limitless decorative effects.

Generally, embroidered paper will be attached to another surface. Consider a variety of glues and adhesives for finishing paper projects, such as double-stick tape, spray glue, fusible web, scrapbooking glue stick, eyelets, brads, decorative staples and ordinary white craft glue.

Embroidery

When embroidering on paper, you may not hoop the paper. Instead, hoop adhesive stabilizer and attach the paper to it. Exceptions can be made for paper that will be trimmed to size after embroidery, cutting away the hoop marks, and for soft papers that can be pressed with an iron after embroidery to remove the marks.

Be sure to stabilize any paper for additional support both during and after embroidery. Use a light spray of temporary adhesive if necessary when using non-adhesive stabilizers. Be cautious about using water-activated adhesives, since the damp stabilizer could cause the paper dye to spot or fade.

To mark an embroidery location, use a pin to make a tiny prick at the embroidery center, or make very light pencil marks that can be erased later. If the motif center is completely filled, the center mark will be covered by embroidery, hiding any marks behind the finished design.

After embroidery, carefully remove the stabilizer by cutting away the excess or gently tearing the stabilizer while supporting and protecting the stitches with the fingers of your other hand. Stabilizers, especially adhesive varieties, can remain behind the embroidered paper motif, even if the stabilizer is a tear-away (usually considered temporary). The stabilizer adds body and durability to the paper.

Rules Are Made to Be Broken

Use vellum or other papers with a large needle (100/16, or a wing needle) to make a perforated paper design. Hoop the paper wrong side up without stabilizer, or with an adhesive stabilizer attached to the paper wrong side. Stitch a simple open design without thread. The result is a pattern of raised holes on the paper's right side.

Trim away the excess paper after embroidery to eliminate the hoop marks. It's a great way to create a lampshade or decorative holiday luminarias.

Stitch an outline of very short stitches with an unthreaded needle around the edge of an embroidered motif. The stitches will perforate the paper, creating an embroidered cutout shape.

Criswell Embroidery & Design, Holiday Embroidery on Paper/Wood 2004 Sampler

Go ahead and embroider on brittle papers. Just plan ahead and use an adhesive stabilizer backing that becomes a permanent part of the project.

Instead of embroidering a frame for a photo, print the photo on art paper and embroider the frame around it. You can also add embroidered embellishments to any photograph this way: a clown hat on your brother, butterflies on a garden snapshot, etc.

My Fair Lady Designs, Wedding Stipple Set 1

And for a truly wild and wacky idea, why not combine embroidered fabric embellishments with paper to create a finished project?

Project Possibilities

Use embroidery on scrapbook pages in a variety of ways:

- ~ Small embroidered embellishments to stick on the page
- ~ Embroidered borders on page edges
- ~ Mats for photographs — use framing shapes, or make a partial mat from two or four corner motifs

Use similar ideas to create unique cards for any occasion. Either embroider the card itself, or embroider a separate piece of paper and attach it to the card.

You can also embroider envelopes and postcards. Yes, they're mailable! Visit www.usps.com for more information on size regulations and postage rates.

Another option is to create gift bags, tags and boxes.

Linda Says

If the paper rips or the embroidery splits the paper, it may still be possible to use the design. Try to push the stitches back into place with your fingers, and secure them with an adhesive stabilizer or tape patch applied to the wrong side.

Husqvarna Viking, Mini-Sampler

If the perforation causes an entire design area to fall away from the paper (for example, the center of the middle flower shown in the photo), you may find you've added an interesting detail to the design and simply leave it as is!

Pocket Toppers

Adding fun to a child's (or a child-at-heart's) garment is easy when you choose from the many pocket toppers available. These clever gems sit above the pocket and add just a subtle (or not so subtle) touch of whimsy to even the traditional work attire.

Use the design and follow the instructions on the enclosed CD-ROM to embroider this pocket topper on your own garment.

Topper Talk

Pocket toppers can have many themes — from sports, nature, hobbies, occupations and cartoon characters to just plain silliness. They're proportioned to fit the width of an adult or child's shirt pocket, and often the lower edge is straight to just barely tuck into the pocket hemline.

The goal of positioning true pocket toppers is to have them appear to be emerging from the pocket space, so placement is critical. If the motif floats above the pocket opening, it's OK, but it's not a topper in the strictest sense.

Some pocket toppers also have additional parts, so animals can appear to be hanging onto or coming through the patch pocket. Others actually go around the pocket corner, necessitating exact placement so as not to stitch down the pocket corner or top.

Sneaky Stitching

If you're very careful, you won't have to take the pocket off of a ready-made garment to add a topper.

1. Make a full-size template of the embroidery motif and mark the design center point. If necessary, use embroidery software to adjust the design size to fit an existing pocket.

2. Mark the pocket width center point at the upper edge. Although most pocket toppers are centered across the pocket opening, that's not an absolute — if the design warrants it, or you want to combine the topper with additional motifs or lettering, place it accordingly.

3. Place the template over the pocket upper edge, centering if desired, with the design lower edge just below the upper pocket edge. Keep the design lower edge parallel to the pocket upper edge.

4. Mark the design center point and hoop alignment markings. Since placement is critical for pocket toppers, double check the marking positions before stitching. Remember, the goal is to have no gap between the lower edge of the embroidery and the pocket upper edge.

5. Turn the upper pocket edge to the right side and tape or pin it out of the way to avoid getting it caught in the embroidery. On very small garments, you may need to remove the pocket stitching for about ½" down each side for access.

6. Hoop the garment with the stabilizer, aligning the placement markings with the hoop markings. *Note:* Use a stabilizer that is compatible with the garment weight. Shirts made from suede, corduroy or any fabric with surface pile will need a topper to keep the design from sinking into the fabric surface. Depending on the garment configuration, it may be helpful to use the rotation or mirror-image function on your embroidery machine to position the design accurately.

Oops!

OESD, CI220/Mellisa Karlin Mahoney photo

If your pocket topper doesn't tuck into the pocket top, don't despair — add some satin stitching in a matching thread color across the stitching lower edge to extend it into the pocket. Or, if it's appropriate for the motif, add a row of trim, rickrack, etc. to lengthen the motif. The trim can be extended beyond the pocket width to look purposeful.

Printing

Heart: OESD, NV745/The Vintage Workshop, Creative Cardmaking Click-n-Craft CD-ROM(V312)–Days We Celebrate

Printing fabric is incredibly fun, and you can use your own photos, create text or choose from ready-to-print images as the basis for your creations, accenting the printed pieces with machine embroidery.

Cactus Punch, Vintage Aircraft

First Things First

Always do the printing *before* the embroidery. It is possible to run embroidered fabric through the printer, but the stitched portions will become blobs of ink!

Print your project on pre-treated natural-fiber fabrics to help maintain permanency during washing. Commercially treated fabrics are available in several weaves and weights, or prepare your own using a product called Bubble Jet Set.

Pre-treated fabrics come with a paper backing to carry the fabric through the printer rollers. If you make your own printable fabrics, use full-sheet, self-adhesive sticky labels on the back side as the carrier.

Image Options

Anything you can print from your computer onto paper can also be printed onto fabric. Several companies sell images on CD-ROMs with pre-sized options. Others offer JPEG imagery so you can make changes in image-editing software.

Your own photos and purchased stock photography are also options for printing, as is clip-art. Use a scanner to create your own artwork or scan images into the computer.

Print Pointers

- Test-print the image on paper before you print the fabric. Make any adjustments needed to alter size, brightness, color, etc. using a graphics editing program, and check the positioning on the page for the intended use.
- Print a full-size template of your embroidery design to check location and fit with the image you plan to print.
- Check the printable fabric to be sure there are no stray threads or lint on the surface, as these act as a resist and will leave unprinted spots once they're removed.
- Also check for frayed areas around the fabric edges, as loose threads can get caught in the printer rollers.
- Moisture in the air may cause prepared fabric sheets to curl, but a quick pressing from the paper side is all that's needed to make them flat again.
- Place one sheet of fabric in the printer tray at a time with the fabric side in the proper direction for feeding and printing.
- Check the printer properties settings and adjust to "normal quality" and "plain paper" settings.
- Once the fabric is printed, follow the manufacturer's instructions to remove the backing and for any post-printing treatment needed. These vary by brand.

The Embroidery Tie-In

If you're printing a small image, print it in the center of the fabric sheet to allow extra at the edges for hooping. If you're printing a large image, it may be necessary to add on extra fabric to allow for hooping, or use a non-hooping method.

Mark the design center location using a pin or small chalk dot. It's best not to use a water-soluble marker unless the center mark will be covered. Inkjet printed images are prone to water-spotting, and wetting can leave permanent marks on your project.

Treat the printed fabric just as you would any other embroiderable fabric base. Select a stabilizer appropriate to the fabric weight and type. If there isn't enough fabric to hoop around your print, use spray adhesive to hold your print to the hooped stabilizer, or use a hooped adhesive stabilizer.

Inspiration

The world is your oyster for combining embroidery with printed imagery …
- Add stitched corners to photos or make entire embroidered frames.
- Use text to add photo captions or titles.
- Personalize a quilt label with a photo of the creator and add the relevant information (date, name, recipient, etc.) with embroidery, or use embroidered borders around printed fabric information.
- Add an embroidered motif to a printed recipe, poem or quote.
- Don't forget that the printed image itself can be accented with embroidery. Add a bouquet of flowers to a bride's hands or a character on a child's solid-color shirt.
- Either the embroidery or the image can take prominence in your project. Just remember to keep the motif in proportion to the image.

Cactus Punch, Quosy Quilter

Some embroidery resources have created printable designs that incorporate embroidery into them. Printable PDF files come with marked locations for the pre-sized stitch motifs.

Quilting In The Hoop

Quilters know that foundation piecing is the way to accurate and consistent piecing, producing perfect results time after time. Traditionally, the foundations are printed or traced onto paper, fabric or tear-away stabilizer, and the only obstacles to accuracy are the distortions introduced by the printer or tracer. Digitizing the foundation design removes those obstacles and assures consistency throughout multiple copies of a single block.

LJI Designs, Foundation Quilt Blocks, 2" Log Cabin, courtesy of Creative Machine Embroidery

Enclosed CD-ROM, AutoBlok

Use the design and follow the instructions on the enclosed CD-ROM to create this quilt.

Material Concerns

When learning to foundation piece, use the 100-percent cotton fabrics readily associated with quilting for the best results. Once you have mastered the technique (a simple process!), this method becomes an excellent way to incorporate unusual fabrics such as velvet, brocades, lamés and satins into quilt blocks.

Cotton thread is the usual choice for piecing, since its fiber content and strength most likely match the fabric used. However, polyester and blended threads are also acceptable, and their added strength may be a plus with tear-away foundations. Fine machine sewing threads (60- or 80-weight) reduce seamline bulk for best results with pieces as small as ¼".

Although the digitized design shows multiple thread colors, the same color is used throughout. Choose a neutral shade (white, black, gray or beige) that blends with the fabrics. Use the same thread in both needle and bobbin unless your machine produces more consistent tension with embroidery bobbin thread.

Here's an inspirational variety of plain and embellished blocks, all pieced in the hoop.

Husqvarna Viking, Cards 130 and 147/Decker Design Studio, Crazy about Krazy Patch/Designs in Stitches, Candlewicking, courtesy of Sew News

Needles for foundation piecing must pierce multiple fabric and stabilizer layers. A size 75/11 embroidery needle usually works, but switch to a sharp needle, size 80/12 or 90/14, if skipped stitches are a problem.

In machine-embroidered foundation piecing, stabilizer takes the place of the foundation paper or fabric. Lightweight cut-away stabilizer is a good choice when assembling projects without batting or when using unusual or unstable fabrics for patches (as in traditional crazy quilts). You can use muslin or batiste as a permanent foundation layer, too. With either of these two options (fabric or permanent stabilizer), the foundation remains with the pieced block in the finished project.

More often, however, the foundation needs to be removed after the block is pieced. Water-soluble stabilizer is an excellent option for blocks constructed with cotton calicoes and quilting fabrics, since it disappears completely. Once the stabilizer is removed, the pieced block is identical in appearance and texture to a traditionally pieced example. Tear-away stabilizer is another possibility, but take care to avoid distorting the stitches and patch edges as you remove it. Choose a thin tear-away to avoid leaving loose stitches.

Firm Foundations

You don't need templates to cut patches for foundation piecing. Instead, draw — or in the case of machine embroidery, stitch — the block seamlines on the foundation and use them as guides for seaming the block. This sewing-on-the-lines method leads to unparalleled accuracy.

In some cases, the block instructions include measurements for cutting individual patches. This simplifies the task of positioning new patches as the block grows. Even so, exact cutting is unnecessary, and the instructions frequently list fabric strip widths rather than dimensions for a patch shape.

Although individual digitizers may vary the process, the basic method for machine-embroidered foundation piecing is the same. The seamlines are converted to digitized running stitches with embroidery software, and the fabric patches are assembled on a layer of hooped stabilizer. The design itself resembles abstract artwork, since each seamline appears in a different color to ensure the machine stops between steps.

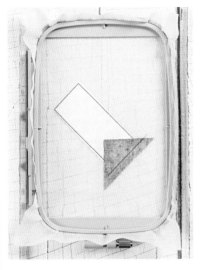

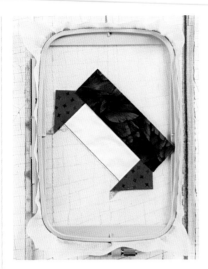

1. To piece a block in the embroidery hoop, begin by hooping a layer of stabilizer. Stitch the first color stop to locate the placement of the first fabric patch.

3. Lay Patch 2 on top of Patch 1, right sides together. Stitch the next portion of the design to seam the two patches. Fold Patch 2 into position on the stabilizer and finger-press the seam. Trim if directed, and use a dot of fabric glue to hold the patch in place on the stabilizer if necessary.

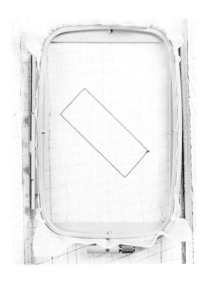

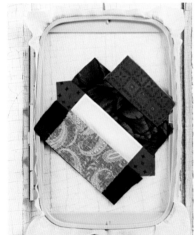

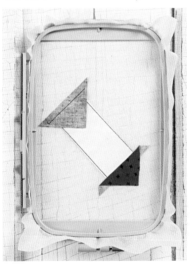

2. Lay the Patch 1 fabric face up on the foundation and stitch the second color to secure the patch. Trim the patch edges if directed to do so.

4. Lay Patch 3 on the previously sewn patches, right sides together, and stitch the next seam. Fold Patch 3 into place on the stabilizer as in Step 3.

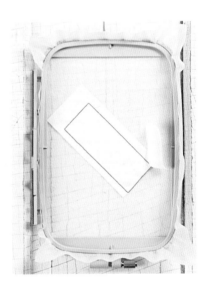

5. Continue adding patches until the block is complete. The last seam will be a basting line around the block perimeter to hold the patch edges in place.

6. Remove the stabilizer and block from the hoop. Follow the digitizer's instructions to trim the block outer edges. In some cases, the basted perimeter may be the cutting line; in others, trim about ¼" outside the basting to create the block seam allowance.

Try This

- Use foundation piecing to create pre-quilted blocks. Simply substitute batting for the foundation stabilizer, or add a layer of lightweight batting on top of the stabilizer as you hoop.
- Add machine embroidered designs to the pieced block. Stitch small motifs inside the patches, or add large quilting motifs that cross the patch seams. You can also use decorative machine stitches or digitized stitch patterns to embellish the block seamlines.
- Digitize your own foundation patterns. Since there are no fill stitches, foundations are an uncomplicated digitizing task. Scan the block pattern into the computer or draw the seamlines within the digitizing program. Remember to assign each seam a different color, so the machine stops to allow fabric placement.
- Re-size for multiple blocks. Once the foundation is digitized, the only limiting factor is hoop size. Enlarge the foundation to a 7" square or work in miniature by decreasing it to 2". You can even make a square block into a rectangle in customizing software! Always test-stitch to be sure the stitch length is still appropriate after re-sizing.
- Combine in-hoop piecing with in-hoop sewing to make a quick coaster. After piecing and before basting, cover the pieced block with another fabric patch. Place right sides together. Stitch the basting, remove from the hoop, and trim a scant ¼" outside the basting. Remove a few stitches from the basted outline and turn the coaster right-side out through the opening. Close the opening with hand stitches and press the coaster to complete.

This school of multi-size fish demonstrates the flexibility of in-hoop piecing. Simply re-size the embroidery design to create blocks in different sizes.

"Embroidery Machine Essentials: Quilting Techniques," courtesy of Sew News

Reflective Film

Mylar is a strong polyester film that was developed along with other polyester fibers in the 1950s. It can be aluminized to create a shiny surface, but unlike aluminum and tin foils, Mylar does not tear easily.

Film Stars

Familiar uses of Mylar are shiny gift-wraps, helium balloons and videotapes. It also makes an excellent and interesting topper for machine embroidery. Designs created with a Mylar underlay can be machine washed, but should not be dry-cleaned. After many washings, the Mylar may lose some of its luster.

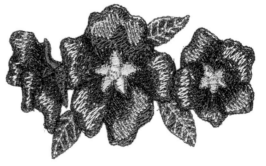

To stitch with Mylar, begin with a low-density design. Some motifs are available with low-density fills, sometimes in combination with regular density versions of the same designs. Regular density designs can be converted to lower density by simply enlarging the motif without

changing the stitch count. Increasing the motif size about 20 percent while maintaining the stitch count spreads the threads farther apart, allowing the Mylar to shine through. Some embroidery machines have this capability, or you can use a re-sizing or customizing software package.

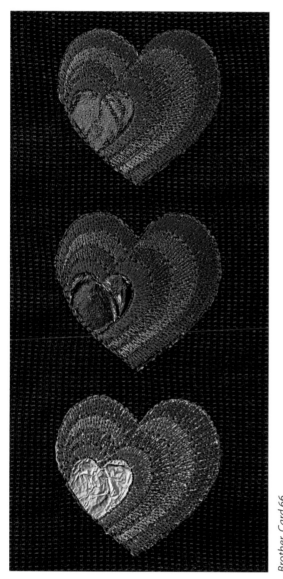

The same motif stitched with three different colors of Mylar.

Computer software may also allow you to alter the fill density while leaving running and satin stitches unchanged for a neater finished appearance. If altering the density without changing the design size, lower the density setting to about 65 percent.

1. When the design is ready, hoop the stabilized fabric and lay a piece of Mylar large enough to cover the embroidery area on the fabric.

Brother, Card 66

The same motif stitched with (top) and without (bottom) a Mylar underlayer.

2. Stitch the motif in one or several thread colors. The Mylar film need not match the thread color; in fact, using a contrasting color underlay is one way to change the design appearance.

3. Before the outline is sewn, remove the hoop from the machine and carefully trim the Mylar just outside the embroidered fill. Return the hoop to the machine and finish stitching.

4. If any bits of Mylar remain visible outside the embroidery, color them with a permanent marker to match the outline thread color.

Amazing Designs Sensational Series, Asian Mylar Magic

Try Angelina instead of Mylar for another take on low-density underlays. See A — Angelina on page 14 for more details.

Brother, Card 66

89

Screen

There are a variety of screening materials on the market for outdoor use as picnic accessories, tote bags, book bags, food covers, swimsuit holders, etc. and you can embroider on them all, if they are synthetic. For a bit of whimsy, embroider fun bugs on your screen door!

Look for a myriad of colors and mesh styles. Your home improvement store has the basics of black, gray and beige, but an awning/tent company, fabric store or even your local quilt shop may have brightly colored offerings by the roll or pre-cut piece. Pet stores often sell a heavy mesh called pet screening. Embroider only on synthetic screening (fiberglass, nylon or polyester), not metal!

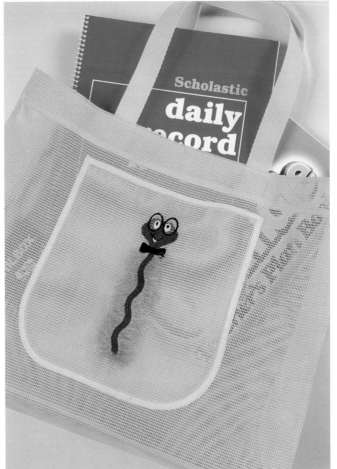

Enclosed CD-ROM, Bookworm

Use the design and follow the instructions on the enclosed CD-ROM to try your hand at embroidery on screen with this handy book bag.

Under and Over

The key to screen embroidery success is to use a totally removable stabilizer to avoid show-through. Water-soluble stabilizer works well for this purpose. For heavy screening, use a heavier weight of stabilizer or multiple layers of a lightweight one.

Test-stitch a screen sample to determine the design integrity. If the stitching sinks into the screening, add a layer of water-soluble stabilizer to the screen surface and try again. This topper helps to keep the stitches above the screen surface and avoids the distortion caused by stitching sinking into the mesh structure.

To embroider a light color over dark screen, use a colored vinyl topper as a barrier to keep the screen color from showing through the design. The topper color should match the predominant thread color of the embroidery motif.

Embroidery

1. If your screen ravels, tape the edges to avoid damage during the embroidery process.

2. If you are embroidering on a large section of screening, roll up the excess and secure with ties or bike clips to make the embroidery process easier. It's not a good idea to hoop screening, as it can cause permanent distortion and damage to the mesh. *Note:* Embroider small screen project sections separately before assembling.

3. Mark the design placement center marks with pins, as actually marking on screen is tricky. Use the woven grid lines to aid in placing the screen in the hoop.

4. Hoop water-soluble stabilizer and spray it with temporary adhesive. Finger-press the screen in place, aligning the woven mesh lines with the hoop placement lines.

5. Spray a piece of water-soluble stabilizer and place it on top of the screen covering the design area if your test-stitching determined a topper is necessary.

6. Use a small size needle to avoid puncturing the screen structure.

7. Since the screen is see-through, match the bobbin thread to the color of the motif edge stitching.

8. When the embroidery is complete, rinse away the stabilizer, following the manufacturer's instructions.

Enclosed CD-ROM, Deccircl; Plate: Clotilde

Just A Thought

Clear View

Who would have thought that you'd be eating on top of your embroidery? Pop the back off of this clever plate and insert an embroidered motif. Just put the back on to protect your stitchery.

Smocking

Fancy Folding

Machine embroidery can be used to duplicate the appearance of traditional smocked panels, those waves and diamonds that patient mothers have long stitched for their children's clothes. The secret lies in pleating the fabric before embroidery, just as hand embroiderers do.

Use the multiple needles and threads of a smocking pleater to gather a section of fabric wide enough to accommodate the embroidery design. A pleater is a device consisting of a roller and multiple threaded needles. By passing the fabric through the roller mechanism, the user can quickly and simply produce consistent pleats across the fabric width. Pull up the gathering threads to bring the fabric to the correct width for your project. If no pleater is available, pleat the fabric by marking a series of regular dots and connecting them with gathering stitches (iron-on transfers are available for this process). Heirloom sewing shops may offer pleating services for a fee. It's also possible to simulate the effect of smocking pleats by stitching regularly-spaced rows of long machine stitches, but the pleats will not be as sharp and regular as those created with a pleater.

Deb Yedziniak, The Diamonds Galore Collection

Deb Yedziniak, The Diamonds Galore Collection

When pleating for hand smocking, contrasting thread is used so the lines of gathering stitches can serve as placement guides for embroidery stitches. The pleating threads are easily removed when stitching is complete. In machine embroidered smocking, it is difficult to remove the pleating threads after embroidery, so use thread that matches the fabric.

Steady Sewing

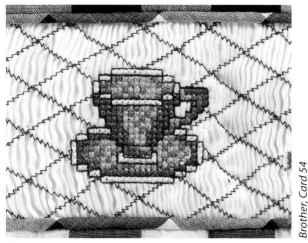

Brother, Card 54

1. Hoop a length of adhesive stabilizer and expose or activate its sticky surface.

2. Attach the pleated fabric, smoothing the pleats into regularity as you go. If the smocked design requires more than one hooping, stabilize and embroider one hoop-size section at a time. Generally, the work begins at one end of the smocked area, but it may be useful to begin in the middle and work toward both ends if the design needs to be centered in the finished project.

3. To keep the embroidery foot from catching the pleats and gathering threads as you stitch, cover the pleated fabric with a layer of lightweight water-soluble stabilizer. Use the machine's basting function to sew around the hoop perimeter, holding all the fabric and stabilizer layers in place.

4. Once the embroidery is finished, remove the stabilizer.

Deb Yedziniak, The Diamonds Galore Collection

Finishing Touches

For a neat finished appearance, lay the pleated and embroidered fabric facedown on a padded ironing surface. Reshape the pleats and pin the fabric edges to the ironing board. Hold a steam iron just above the fabric surface so the steam penetrates the pleats. Allow to dry before removing the pins, and your smocking is complete.

Traditional geometric designs aren't the only ones appropriate for stitching on pleated fabric. Use cross stitch or other motifs to simulate the look of picture smocking. And smocking designs don't have to be stitched on pleated fabric! Their geometric regularity is appealing on flat fabric, too, or stitch the same design on both flat and pleated fabrics for a beautifully coordinated set.

Soap

What's the perfect accompaniment for embroidered toilet paper (see T — Toilet Paper on page 96)? Stitched soap!

EmbroideryArts, Art Deco 3

Embroidered soap is good, clean fun.

Dirty Details

1. Look for a bar of soap with a flat surface — no embossed logo.

2. Unwrap the soap and lay it face down on a wet sponge in a shallow dish of water. Leave it there to soften while you embroider.

3. Hoop a layer of water-soluble film with a layer of tulle or organza that matches the soap.

4. Stitch a small, filled motif or a simple one-letter monogram.

5. Remove from the hoop and trim away the stabilizer and fabric close to the embroidery.

8. Paint over the soap and embroidery with a thin coat of melted paraffin wax to protect the surface. The soap, like the toilet paper, is for looking only. Enjoy!

Shamrock, Hearts: Husqvarna Viking, Mini-Sampler; Holly: OESD, NV732/Mellisa Karlin Mahoney photo

Tip

You may not need to trim the fabric from small areas inside the embroidery; for example, the hole in the letter "A" should disappear into the soap surface.

6. Lift the soap off the sponge and lay it, softened side up, on your work surface. Arrange the embroidery on the soap, face up, and press it firmly into the soap surface. Mist the surface with water to dissolve any stabilizer still visible around the embroidery.

7. Cover the embroidered surface with plastic wrap for about an hour. The soap will work its way between the threads to hold the design in place. Remove the plastic wrap and allow the soap to dry completely.

Just A Thought

Try to Remember

Use a fine-point permanent marker to label bobbins that contain unusual or specialty threads, such as water-soluble or shrinkable. Many of these novelty threads are white and hard to distinguish from one another.

Toilet Paper

*W*hen friends ask us about the rationale for embroidering on toilet paper, the answer comes back to the premise of this book — "because you can." Why would you want to? Clearly it's not because someone would really use your TP handiwork for its intended purpose — heaven forbid!

Embroidered toilet paper looks great in a guest bathroom basket with soaps, towels, etc. Tie it up in some tulle or organza with ribbons and see if people question this unique accent when they come out of this all-important room. It's also great to leave out for parties or special holidays and makes a fun addition to a housewarming basket. If you're a real estate agent, what could be more personal than a gift at closing with a house motif and the new address?

On a Roll

Choose high-quality toilet paper and look for the two-ply labeling. Single-ply doesn't have enough body to support the stitching.

As with all paper embroidery, choose a design that doesn't have dense stitch coverage. If you have editing skills, eliminate underlay stitches. Use editing software or on-screen functions to enlarge the design to reduce thread density. Redwork motifs and quilt outlines are perfect for TP, as the stitch count is usually low compared to filled designs.

If you want to keep the tissue attached to the roll while you embroider, you may need a partner-in-crime to assist. Another option is to detach several sheets from the roll and later wrap it around the outside before displaying or covering the roll for gift-giving.

Embroidery

1. Pull off a considerable length from the toilet paper roll so that you have flexibility for the embroidery process.

2. Use a new, small-size needle — size 65/9 or 70/10 — to avoid creating large holes in the paper.

3. Stabilizing the paper is important, otherwise even the finest quality TP will end up in shreds. Create a sandwich from the toilet tissue and water-soluble stabilizer. Never fear — you won't be using water to remove the stabilizer! Fold over two or three sheets of TP, align the edges and mark the design center point with a tiny dot of air-soluble marker. Place water-soluble stabilizer on top and under the stacked sheets, then hoop gently, leaving the extended paper attached to the roll.

4. Place the hoop on the embroidery arm and set the TP roll to the side or behind the machine with a generous extension of paper so that it doesn't tear off during the embroidery process. If your sewing surface doesn't allow for this positioning, ask a friend to hold the roll and give you slack between.

5. Embroider the design, then gently tear away the water-soluble stabilizers.

Tip

Oh, Poop! If you ruin the embroidery for some reason, just tear off the sheets and start over.

Finishing the Job

Wrap the paper back on the roll so it looks like it came that way. Add it to a basket on the bathroom counter or the back of the toilet, or wrap it in tulle, net or organza and tie up the ends with ribbons. The most fun — seeing the reaction of the guests or the recipient!

Just A Thought

Water, Water Everywhere

Whether we realize it or not, moisture is part of our everyday atmosphere. Some areas have more moisture in the air than others.

Keep water-soluble thread in a sealed plastic bag in a dry area to avoid deterioration in high-humidity areas. Mark the bag with an identifying label to avoid mixing up the dissolvable thread with other embroidery offerings, as the appearance is similar.

Moisture on your hands and steam pressing can also affect the water-soluble stabilizer — both can cause the thread to become sticky.

Unusual Threads

Several novelty threads are available. Experiment using these ideas and techniques to add a little something extra to your embroidery motifs.

Glow-in-the-Dark Thread

After exposure to natural or artificial light, specially treated glow-in-the-dark threads will hold their luminescence for up to 15 hours.

There are differences between brands, but this specialty thread is available in 30-, 35- or 40-weights. Made from polyester or polypropylene, look for white, peach, lime green, yellow, blue, purple and pink. All glow eerily under black light or in the dark.

Glow-in-the-dark thread is washable (without bleach) in cool water, and some brands are machine dryable on low temperatures. It shouldn't be ironed directly, but it can be pressed with a pressing cloth.

What a Haunt!

Perhaps the most obvious use for glow-in-the-dark thread is for Halloween costumes, totes, masks and decorations, but don't stop there. Think about other fun uses as well — embroidered stars for a child's bedroom ceiling, notes stitched on pillowcases for kids or newlyweds, switch plates and love notes penned on pjs or boxers, or sweet sentiments on a bedside lamp shade. Because of the long-lasting glow, this novelty thread is often used on outerwear for safety. Motifs can be stitched on bike wear, jogging clothes and even

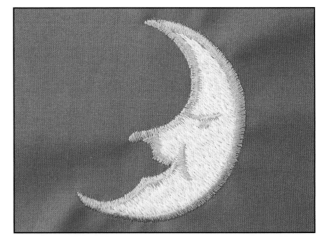

Look for surprise elements when the lights go out!

Anita Goodesign, Halloween

pet accessories to increase visibility. The glow isn't affected by moisture, so you'll shine even walking in the rain or snow.

Sew What

You may need to loosen the thread tension slightly to work with glow-in-the-dark threads, but your test-stitching will tell the tale. Use a standard needle and stabilizer as you would for a comparable weight thread of the non-glow variety. Some machines work better using a slower speed than normal.

Remember, motifs that are heavily filled with stitching (thread) show up more than simple outline designs when the lights go out.

Metallic Magic

Combine metal with glow-in-the-dark characteristics and you'll have double shine. Look for Brilliance metallic thread from YLI for this incredible combination.

Rebecca Says

Some glow-in-the-dark threads are heavy enough to pile up in filled areas of a motif. Test-stitch first and reduce the design density using software — or enlarge the design without changing the stitch count — to allow enough space for the thicker thread.

Another fun use for these threads: Stitch a motif on towels for a guest bathroom, to greet visitors even during the night!

Just A Thought

Incredible Shrinking Thread

Enclosed CD-ROM, DecCircl

Chi-zi-mi bobbin thread is formulated to shrink on contact with heat, producing an effect similar to smocking. Try it with machine embroidery designs to create unusual and nifty special effects. Choose running stitch or outline-only motifs. Experiment with grid designs, swirls and quilting designs. Use a regular thread in the needle, in a color that matches or contrasts with the fabric.

Apply a hot iron and lots of steam. The thread shrinks almost immediately, then stabilizes and will shrink no more. In the finished product, the embroidery design becomes secondary to the bubbly texture. Use the motifs to create textured fabric for a collar, cuff or pocket, or scatter spots of texture across an entire garment.

Solar-Reactive Thread

Indoors

Outdoors

Here comes the sun … and also a change in your embroidery motif, if you used solar-reactive thread. Made of polypropylene, this novelty thread made by SolarActive International is 40-weight and can be stitched as you would any standard embroidery thread of the same weight. Some machines require a looser tension to keep the bobbin thread from showing on the colorful side.

There are two types of solar-reactive threads available — those that start out white and change to a pastel color, and those that start out colored and change to a different color. Of the latter grouping, peach changes to wine, turquoise to blue, yellow to orange and pink to magenta. So, keep the color change in mind as you choose a color for embroidery motif sections.

How's it Work?

The chemistry of the thread is, of course, a trade secret, but we do know that several factors affect the color transformation.

Climate greatly affects the color changing speed and duration; thread colors are more intense in cold climates than in warm. The ozone level also affects the life of the color changing ability. In most climate zones, the UV rays are strongest at mid-day when the sun is directly overhead. When the stitching is removed from the sunlight, the color slowly dissipates, returning to its original hue. Yellow, orange and red take the longest to fade.

Designed to withstand about 2,000 launderings — more than the lifespan of a normal garment — the solar-reactive thread is washable on cool or warm temperature settings without bleach, and can be dried on a low temperature setting. Bleaching will destroy the color changing abilities, as will any heat over 420 degrees. Don't iron directly on the thread — press from the project wrong side.

Prolonged exposure to sunlight will also zap the color changing abilities from the thread in short order. To extend the color-changing properties, store the project (and your thread spools) out of the light.

Sunny Stitching

Solar-reactive thread is great fun, especially for kids' embroidery, as they have a great fascination with the color changing. Use it for any type of outdoorwear embellishing: beach towels, hats, cover-ups, ski wear, sport totes, garden aprons and totes, banners and picnic cloths. If you use it on children's clothing, be prepared for the inside-outside frenzy as they activate the color changes. Children's toys are also fun to embroider with this novelty thread. It's non-toxic, so never fear if toy eating or sucking is involved.

Any kind of celebration that moves from indoors to outdoors is fair game for solar-reactive thread. An all-white embroidered wedding dress becomes even more special when it blooms full color at the outdoor reception. Sunrise services have extra punch when the clergy's stole changes color as the sun appears. Proms, pool parties and office parties are perfect occasions for solar-reactive thread embellishment projects — people take a second look, not believing their eyes.

Don't forget your favorite pet — stitch on leashes, collars and coats.

Tip

When using the white-to-pastel solar-reactive thread, consider mixing it with traditional embroidery thread so that the motif has some color indoors as well.

Vinyl Embroidery

If you plan to embroider directly on vinyl, be sure to use the smallest needle possible to avoid large holes — a size 65/9 or 70/10 should support the embroidery thread without leaving a gaping hole.

Enlarge the design, just as you would for paper, metal or other fragile materials, to spread out the needle penetrations. If you have embroidery software, modify the stitch density so the stitching isn't as compact, thus eliminating some perforations.

Match the bobbin thread to the design motif to avoid a contrasting color showing through. This may mean changing the bobbin as you advance color stops if the design has many colors.

Test-stitch to determine if tension adjustments are needed to keep the bobbin threads from showing on the top surface and to keep the vinyl flat after stitching. Too-tight tension can cause distortion.

Hooping (or Not)

Vinyl comes in several weights and colors and can actually be embroidered on or used as an appliqué, creating a window that shows through to the layer below. In addition, knit-back vinyls (think raincoats) add a slick look to an appliqué — some are even textured to look like faux leathers or animal skins.

Look for vinyl at your fabric or craft store — usually with home décor fabrics — and choose a weight depending on the final use, from tote bags to place mats.

We've included three designs on the enclosed CD-ROM that work well with vinyl — the gumball machine/fishbowl, rattle and car, though all can be used with other fabrics as well.

1. Mark the design location center point with a small sticker to avoid marking the vinyl with pin holes or permanent pen. Remove the sticker once the project is positioned and ready for embroidery.

2. *To embroider on a small piece of vinyl,* hoop water-soluble stabilizer and spray with temporary adhesive, then finger-press the vinyl in place.

To embroider on a large piece of vinyl, consider using a non-hooping technique with adhesive stabilizer. Test to be sure the adhesive pulls away from the vinyl without a residue. If not, use removable tape to adhere the vinyl to a tear-away or water-soluble stabilizer.

Use the design and follow the instructions on the enclosed CD-ROM to embroider this car on a T-shirt of your own. Combine clear vinyl for the windshield and colored for the body and bumper.

3. Roll the excess vinyl out of the way and clip or tie in place.

4. To prevent the vinyl from sticking to the machine bed, place a small piece of water-soluble stabilizer underneath the hoop.

5. Once the embroidery is complete, gently pull the vinyl from the hoop and dissolve the stabilizer.

Appliqué

Clear, lightweight vinyl makes intriguing appliqué portions, allowing you to add in things between the vinyl and the base layer. How fun is that?

Think about the potential for a fishbowl with swimming fish and/or "water" (made from fabric of course) inside, or a snowglobe with snowflakes fluttering below, or a car windshield with a peek into the dash. Don't forget about drink glasses filled with your favorite embroidered beverage, a see-through window or a gumball machine with tempting jawbreakers inside. Beads also make a perfect addition under a clear vinyl appliqué.

Fishbowl: Enclosed CD-ROM, Gumball; Cat: Embroidery Central, VB71

Use the design and follow the instructions on the enclosed CD-ROM to create your own fishbowl using vinyl.

Enclosed CD-ROM, RattleLo and RattleUp

Use the design and follow the instructions on the enclosed CD-ROM to create this rattle door hanger.

Clear vinyl windows allow for a look through.

Opaque colored vinyls are also fun. Think yellow taxi, rain slicker or shiny red fire engine. These vinyls have a knit or woven backing which makes them sturdier than their clear counterparts, and not as likely to be damaged by the embroidery process. Some vinyls are embossed with textures to mimic alligator or other animal skin patterns, and they're also perfect for things like footballs, basketballs, etc.

Textured vinyl creates a faux-leather look.

Just A Thought

Shoulder Shapes

Got shoulder pads in your stash and no plans to use them? Make this clever little bag for a kid's coloring kit or your sewing notions. Add a top zipper to close, embroider a motif and sew up the curved edges.

Wood

*E*mbroidering on wood is a surprisingly simple technique guaranteed to amaze and surprise. The secret lies in the material: balsa wood.

Balsa Basics

The lightest wood in the world, balsa is available in strips as thin as $1/32$". Look for it in hobby shops with model building materials or order from Internet sources. Balsa is commonly found in strips 36" long and 3" or 4" wide, with 6" widths available from specialty suppliers. For embroidery, choose $1/16$"- or $1/32$"-thick balsa.

Enclosed CD-ROM, WHeart

Use the design and follow the instructions on the enclosed CD-ROM to make this embroidered box.

Enclosed CD-ROM, WHeartC and WCornerC

Use the design and follow the instructions on the enclosed CD-ROM to make this patchwork tray.

Because balsa splits easily along its grain, use care when handling and storing the strips. Also keep the limitation of strip width in mind as you choose motifs to embroider. With advance planning, you can create a patchwork of wooden squares as the basis for larger projects.

Supplies

In addition to the balsa wood, you'll need a few basic supplies: stabilizer, threads, needles and materials for finishing the project.

Choose an adhesive stabilizer with a protective paper covering for wood embroidery. Unlike water-activated adhesive stabilizers, this type provides a strong bond distributed evenly over its entire surface. The stabilizer becomes a permanent part of the project and serves to strengthen and stabilize the wood as well as the embroidery design.

Additional tear-away stabilizer is needed for most embroidery on wood. Select a stabilizer that tears easily after embroidery and has enough body to slide under the hooped stabilizer and wood.

An embroidery needle, size 75/11, is the right choice for stitching on wood. It is small enough to penetrate the wood easily without leaving a large hole. With wood embroidery, it is wise to replace the needle when the project is finished — before stitching your next project on fabric.

The soft balsa is unlikely to damage the needle, but the combination of wood and stabilizer adhesive may dull the needle or coat it with sticky residue. Keep a needle cleaning packet or alcohol swabs handy and clean the needle frequently during embroidery.

Most threads are suitable for wood embroidery, although fragile metallic threads may shred while passing through the wood's thickness. Switching to a topstitching needle designed to protect larger threads while sewing may help, but ultimately some specialty threads may be unsuitable for embroidery on wood.

Wood embroidery projects are usually mounted on a wood or fabric base to finish the wrong side and support the lightweight balsa. For finishing you will need glue; cutting tools (a rotary cutter or craft knife, with mat and ruler); and a box, tray, banner or other item to decorate.

Balsa can also be painted or stained. For best results, apply color to the wood *before* embroidering, and allow time for the paint or stain to dry completely; otherwise the embroidery threads will take on the applied color, too. Stains that sink into the wood are ideal for wood that will be embroidered. Always test surface colors such as paints to be sure they will not crack or chip when penetrated by the embroidery needle, or send flakes into the bobbin works below.

Design Decisions

Most designs can be stitched on wood, but there are a few considerations for best results. Outline-only designs allow the wood surface to show, and can be used as the basis for decorative painting techniques.

Stitches placed along the wood grain sink into the balsa, giving a ragged appearance to the work. This is especially apparent with satin stitch columns, where stitches placed in the direction of the wood grain appear narrow and uneven.

Compare the appearance of the satin stitches along and across the wood grain.

Another drawback to satin stitches: repeated needle penetrations along the edge of a straight column will perforate and separate the balsa, especially when the line of needle holes follows the grain. Rotate the wood 90 degrees so the needle holes run across the grain, or position the motif a few degrees off-grain to avoid the problem.

Enclosed CD-ROM, BookCov2

Use the design and follow the instructions on the enclosed CD-ROM to embroider this cross-stitch motif on wood.

Unlike satin stitches, fill stitches are ideal for wood embroidery since they stagger needle holes across the embroidered shape. Patterned stitches, such as chain stitch or motif fills, also work beautifully on wood. Cross stitch motifs are another attractive choice.

Designs with small stitches or many stitches in a small area may give the wood a chewed appearance. To correct trouble spots, lengthen stitches or decrease the stitch density. Sometimes enlarging the motif without changing the stitch count provides enough space between needle holes to eliminate the problem. If not, save the design for a project on a more traditional base — like fabric!

With any motif stitched on wood, a tension adjustment may be necessary to compensate for the wood thickness. As always, test the chosen motif on scrap wood to assure good project results.

Stitching Time

1. Hoop the adhesive stabilizer sticky-side up. Score the protective paper inside the hoop and remove it to expose the adhesive.

2. Cut a piece of balsa to fit inside the hoop and attach it to the hooped stabilizer. If the wood is larger than the hoop, it will pull away from the stabilizer around the edges, resulting in poor stitch quality, or crack and break as the embroidery progresses. Plan ahead so your project can be constructed from hoop-size pieces.

3. Put the hoop on the machine and slide a piece of tear-away stabilizer under the hoop. Embroider the design.

4. Remove the embroidered wood and stabilizer from the hoop. Working from the wrong side, carefully remove the excess tear-away stabilizer, but leave the adhesive stabilizer intact.

5. Trim the adhesive stabilizer the same size as the balsa. Finger-press firmly to be sure the stabilizer is attached to the entire wood surface for durability.

6. Finish the project by cutting the wood to the desired shape and size. Use white craft glue (high-tack and quick-dry formulations are especially easy to use) to attach the embroidered wood to a box, plaque, felt banner or other base. Cover with a weight to prevent warping and allow to dry completely.

Tips & Ideas

~Balsa strips may come with a sticky label on the back. Don't forget to remove it before embroidering!

~As with metal and paper, holes in wood are permanent. If your embroidery format begins and/or ends each design with a centering stitch, manually skip over these stitches to avoid unwanted holes.

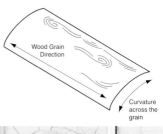

Embroidered balsa can be shaped to wrap around gentle curves like this box lid.

~Balsa can be applied to gently curved surfaces with a little advance planning. While balsa splits easily along its grain, with a backing of adhesive stabilizer it can be carefully curved and shaped. Position the motif so the needed curvature runs across the wood grain. Cut the embroidered wood to the correct size and apply glue evenly to its wrong side. Lay the balsa on the curved foundation and smooth it into place. Use rubber bands to hold the balsa in place as it dries.

~Use embroidered balsa squares for unusual greeting cards. Just trim the wood around the embroidered motif, then glue the square to a handmade or pre-folded card.

~Glue on beads or sequins for added impact.

Troubleshooting

What if an embroidered motif perforates the wood and is in danger of falling out? Handle it carefully as you remove the embroidered wood from the hoop, and gently push the punched area back into place. When the work is glued onto its base, the backing will hold the embroidery in place.

Large designs can cause balsa to ripple, and moisture can warp the porous wood. To repair, glue the embroidered wood to a second piece of balsa the same size. Lay flat and cover with a weight to dry.

Cross Stitch

Machine embroidery duplicates the look of hand cross stitching so successfully, only an expert will know for sure! In fact, several companies that now digitize cross stitch for machine embroiderers began as designers for the hand-cross-stitch market.

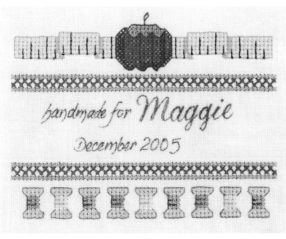

Use the designs and follow the instructions on the enclosed CD-ROM to embroider these cross stitch motifs.

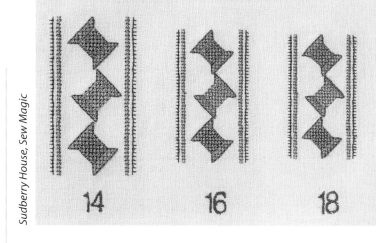

Sudberry House, Sew Magic

14   16   18

Thread Tails

Most machine embroidery cross-stitch motifs are digitized for standard 40-weight embroidery threads. By stitching repeatedly over each part of the cross, the digitizer duplicates the appearance of multi-strand embroidery floss. If you prefer, choose a slightly smaller 50-weight cotton embroidery thread to mimic the look of traditional cotton embroidery floss.

Machine cross stitch also accommodates metallic threads. Just be sure to follow guidelines for stitching with metallics, including using a specialty needle.

For something a bit different, enlarge the cross stitches so there are only six or eight per inch. Stitch the design with a woolly thread for a warm, bulky design especially suited for fleece and heavy fabrics.

Stabilizer Sense

Stabilizer is critical for cross stitching. Each stitch pulls in the same direction, along the fabric's true bias, which can lead to distortion.

Consider the item's end use when you select the stabilizer. If possible, back the fabric with a fusible, cut-away stabilizer or iron-on interfacing, much as you would if embroidering on a knit fabric. Use additional tear-away stabilizer under the hooped fabric, especially for large designs. As always, use the smallest hoop that will accommodate the design for the greatest stability.

Adhesive stabilizers are an attractive option for small items and those that are hard to hoop. They also allow you to reposition the fabric for perfect alignment on an even-weave fabric, or when joining sections to create a very large design. Adhesive stabilizer alone, however, will not support all the stitches of a large cross-stitch motif. Slippage can occur, resulting in the misalignment of later colors and outlines.

Counting Stitches

What does "14-count" mean? Does it matter to a machine embroiderer? "Count" refers to the number of cross stitches in a row 1" long. A 14-count design (14 stitches per inch) will have larger crosses and be larger overall than the same design in 18-count (18 stitches per inch). From a machine embroiderer's point of view, the count only matters in terms of the resulting design size, unless the design is being stitched on an even-weave fabric (more below).

Be cautious about re-sizing machine cross-stitch motifs. Unlike other designs, cross stitch should be re-sized without changing the number of stitches in the design. This means there will still be the same number of crosses, but each one will be larger or smaller. In other words, a 14-count design can be enlarged to a 12-count design, but the number of stitches will stay the same.

Some machine embroidery motifs use cross-shaped stitches without attempting to duplicate their hand-worked cousins. These designs don't rely on a regular repeat, so they have no specific count. Enjoy stitching them on non-even-weave fabrics without worrying about exact stitch size.

In addition, some digitizing programs can produce a fill that mimics cross stitching. These patterns also have no specific count. By adjusting the pattern characteristics, it may be possible to create a fill that looks similar to hand cross stitch.

If you want to digitize your own cross-stitch motifs, look for a cross-stitch program with a machine embroidery add-on to produce the most authentic results.

Fabric Facts

One of the great advantages to machine cross stitch is that it can be worked on almost any fabric. Since there is no need to follow the fabric weave to keep the stitches even (the digitizing takes care of that), machine cross stitch is appropriate for knits, fleece, flannel, denim and many other fabrics.

Sudberry House, Sew Magic

Choose linen and linen-type fabrics to mimic the even-weave materials favored by hand embroiderers. For designs with small stitches (high count numbers, like 18), work on flat fabrics such as broadcloth or fine linen. Larger stitches (low count numbers, like 12) and those with two or three repeats of each stitch are bold enough to work on textured fabrics, sweatshirts and fleece.

Holes in One

Most counted cross stitch (by hand) is worked on even-weave fabrics like Aida cloth. These have the same number of threads per inch in both warp and weft directions, and they may be woven so that the intersecting threads form distinct patterns of fibers and holes. The counted stitches are worked into the holes, providing consistency for the repeated cross stitches.

It's possible to work machine cross stitch on these even-weave fabrics as well, by carefully aligning the fabric yarns while hooping. Be sure the motif count matches the fabric count. If the design doesn't specify the number of stitches per inch, stitch a test sample on plain fabric and count the number of cross stitches in one linear inch. Examine the fabric to be sure the lengthwise and crosswise threads are perpendicular to each other.

1. Most needlework fabrics are heavily sized to keep the grain consistent. Back the fabric with a fusible stabilizer to lock the grain in place and prevent distortion.

2. Hoop the fabric and stabilizer in the smallest hoop that will accommodate the design. If you are using a large hoop, consider hooping additional layers of stabilizer to add more gripping power at the edges; cut away the additional stabilizer underneath the embroidery area before stitching, if desired, to eliminate bulk. Some machine companies sell specially designed padding to boost their hoops' gripping power. *Note:* As you hoop the fabric, be sure the fabric grainlines remain parallel to the hoop sides. If the grain is perpendicular and well-stabilized before hooping, there should be little difficulty. For small items, you may prefer to hoop an adhesive stabilizer and attach the fabric to the adhesive, repositioning the fabric as necessary to perfect the grain.

3. Once the fabric has been accurately hooped, move the needle to the first stitch position. Lower the needle and check to see whether the needle

drops into a hole between fabric threads. If not, use the machine controls to move the design slightly in the hoop so the needle drops correctly.

4. When the needle is correctly positioned, begin to stitch. Like magic, the stitches will fall over the fabric thread intersections — just as if you were stitching by hand!

Stitch slowly. Set your machine for a medium to low speed, especially when stitching outlines around cross-stitch fills. This gives the needle time to slide between the stitches rather than piercing them, for better registration and detail.

Vermillion Stitchery, Christmas Ornaments Collection

Hand or machine? Only an expert knows for sure!

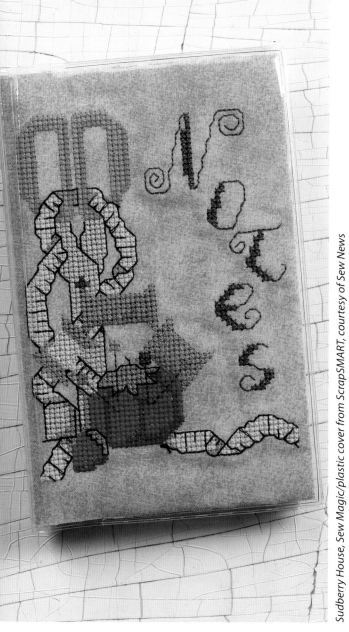

Sudberry House, Sew Magic/plastic cover from ScrapSMART, courtesy of Sew News

Even non-even-weave fabrics are appropriate for machine cross stitch.

Yarn

Yarn is a great addition to embroidery and can be used in many ways. Small yarns can be used in the bobbin and embroidery stitched upside down (see B — Bobbinwork on page 18 for more information). Larger yarns can be used to add hair, fringe and other accents to embroidered motifs, and novelty yarns can be used as portions of a design left unstitched.

Loops

To incorporate yarn into your designs, think of places it's appropriate. Hair on a doll or clown is an ideal place, as is a lion or other animal's mane, tail or portions of its fur. Yarn can also be used for flower loops, held in place with an embroidered center.

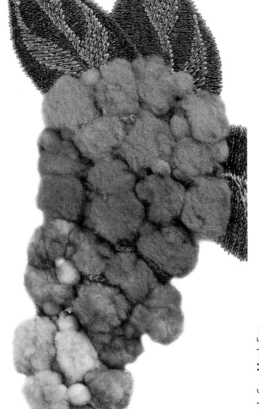

Cactus Punch, Sew Much Fun

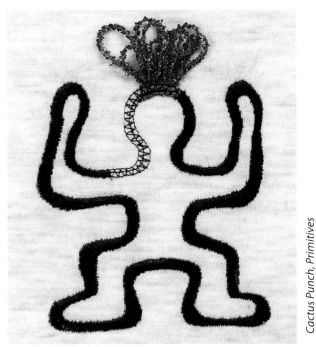

Cactus Punch, Primitives

Underlay stitching catches the yarn loops in place.

The embroidery design underlay stitching catches the yarn loops, holding them securely in place until the finishing stitches cover the yarn ends. To do this, pause the stitching as you get to the area you want to add the yarn, then shape it as desired, overlapping the yarn ends into the embroidery underlay area. To hold multiple loops in place, use tape outside the embroidery area until the stitching is complete.

Another way to combine yarn loops with embroidery is to add them after the embroidery is complete, attaching them with matching or clear thread on the sewing machine, and shaping them individually. Free-motion stitch settings work best for this technique to avoid catching the yarns in the presser foot toes. You can also attach them by hand if you prefer. Check needlework books for information on turkeywork or use a punchneedle embroidery tool.

Novelties

Cactus Punch, Sew Much Fun

This slubby yarn is used to fill in areas that would normally be embroidered.

The yarn market abounds with fun novelty yarns in any color and texture you can imagine. Some yarns are perfect to substitute for portions of an embroidery motif or to add to it after stitching is done. Look for yarns with large slubs, fringed pieces, ribbons, beads and other textural additions for inspiration.

Just A Thought

Moderation for Stability

Follow manufacturers' instructions when fusing stabilizer to fabric. In most cases, a warm iron is all that's needed to activate the fusing agent, and too much heat may strengthen the bond so the stabilizer is difficult to remove.

Similarly, water-activated stabilizers (those you dampen and stick) need just a minimal amount of moisture to hold the fabric during embroidery. Stabilizer that's too wet is difficult to remove; but if you find yourself stuck, re-moistening the stabilizer usually causes it to release from the fabric.

- -

Glitz

Add beads or confetti to embroidery by trapping the additions between layers of sheer organza or tulle, then using the fabric sandwich in place of appliqué fabric or as a background for simple embroidery.

Knitting

This stitched and brushed embroidery has the look and feel of real fur.

What embroidered snowman or animal wouldn't love to sport a hand-knitted scarf or hat? No elaborate knitting skills required; just use fine yarn and knit a square or rectangle, then shape and stitch it onto the embroidered motif.

Try other yarn-crafted options — a knit bag for an embroidered shopper girl, a twisted yarn leash for your favorite embroidered poodle or a blankie for a napping child. Just hand-tack your crafted additions in place after the embroidery is complete!

Don't knit? Experiment with pieces of thrift store sweaters as appliqué embellishments. Use seam sealant or lines of closely spaced straight stitching to keep the cut edges from raveling.

Choose a topstitching needle, size 90/14 or 100/16, and reduce the thread tension to accommodate the larger yarn. Designs must incorporate extra space for the yarn, so look for specially digitized motifs or reduce the density of other designs (see R — Reflective Film on page 88 for more information).

Wool yarn embroidery before and after brushing.

Embroidering with Yarn

Hand embroiderers have used yarn for centuries, and now machine embroiderers can, too. Look for fine wool-blend yarns that have a fluffy finish and are engineered to withstand the stresses of machine embroidery.

Once the embroidery is complete, the fuzzy yarn can be brushed with the hook side of hook-and-loop tape or with a Chenille Brush. The result is truly furry embroidery with a plush hand and soft visual texture.

Just A Thought

Brother, Card 39

Poinsettia People

Embroider small faces on flesh-colored fabric and use it to cover buttons. Replace the centers of large poinsettias or other silk flowers with the button faces by wiring or gluing the covered buttons in place.

Zippers

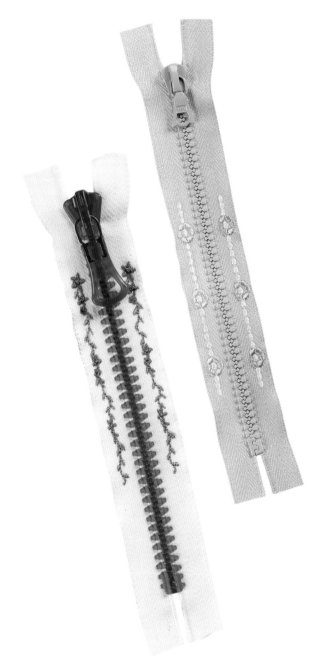

Embroidering on zipper tapes requires a very small design and extremely accurate placement. Look for designs that are less than ½" wide so you can center them on the woven tape, or up to ¾" wide if you want to span the zipper tape and the base fabric.

To be successful with the latter application, the zipper must be applied to the right side of the fabric and the zipper tape must be exposed in the finished item.

Decorative zipper tapes provide the perfect canvas for embroidery.

White zipper: Amazing Designs, Heirloom Floral; Pink/blue zipper: Amazing Designs, Beadwork Collection; Zippers: Riri

Tape Two

To embroider only on a zipper tape — one or both sides — use an adhesive tear-away stabilizer.

1. Activate the stabilizer by removing the protective paper or moistening with water. Either may be done in a relatively narrow area just to secure the zipper tape to the stabilizer.

2. Using a removable marker, mark a center line down the zipper tape and carefully adhere the zipper in place on the stabilizer, aligning the markings with the hoop placement marks. Finger-press the zipper in place.

3. Use the machine's needle-tracing function to be sure the zipper tape is lined up parallel to the stitching line and the design area fits on the tape.

4. Embroider the motif, and then remove the stabilizer before applying the zipper to the project. If you have a long zipper to embellish, rehoop as needed to continue embroidering the required length.

On the Edge

If you prefer to embroider the motif spanning the zipper tape and the base fabric, topstitch the zipper in place first with matching thread, then align the woven edge of the zipper tape with the vertical hoop center for placement and follow the instructions above.

On the Fly

Courtesy of Creative Machine Embroidery

If your zipper is inserted already and you want to add a bit of embroidery pizzazz, think about stitching a message on the fly facing. It's narrow, but you can do it!

It's the perfect place for a secret message to a loved one — like "I ♥ You." For youngsters who might be learning to read, add "front" or "back" to an extra-wide zipper opening seam allowance to help them get dressed, or simply a smiley face to make them laugh.

CD-ROM Contents

Embroidery Design Index

AutoBlok
4.52" x 4.51"
9 thread changes; 1 color

Basket
5.71" x 3.48"
6 colors

Bear
4.28" x 6.32"
5 colors

BearApp
4.28" x 6.32"
5 colors

BobbFull
4.80" x 4.79"
2 colors

BobbQtr
2.41" x 2.41"
1 color

BookCov1
3.90" x 2.89"
11 colors

BookCov2
3.90" x 2.89"
11 colors

BookCov3
3.90" x 2.89"
11 colors

Bookmark
2.34" x 7.47"
7 colors

Bookworm
1.68" x 6.47"
5 colors

CatCollr
3.72" x 0.55"
2 colors

CatFish
1.04" x 0.5
1 color

Chenille
3.86" x 3.86"
1 color

DecCircl
1.25" x 1.25"
1 color

DogBone
0.99" x 0.45"
1 color

DogCollr
3.75" x 0.61"
2 colors

FabBorCo
2.52" x 2.52"
1 color

FabBord
1.98" x 6.67"
1 color

FabricSW
3.86" x 3.84"
3 colors

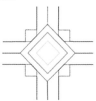

FabStars
3.75" x 3.75"
3 colors

FabSWChn
3.87" x 3.84"
3 colors

FringBor
3.99" x 2.32"
5 colors

Gumball
3.69" x 3.86"
4 colors

Iris
3.81" x 2.03"
2 colors

LindaCar
3.38" x 3.90"
8 colors

MBordCor
2.53" x 2.52"
1 color change; no thread

MetalSW
3.85" x 3.84"
3 color changes; no thread

MetBord
1.98" x 6.69"
1 color change; no thread

MetStars
4.25" x 4.25"
4 color changes; no thread

PendantF
2.58" x 4.23"
5 colors

PendantM
2.58" x 4.23"
5 colors

PFrame
4.74" x 6.39"
3 colors

RattleLo
3.97" x 3.82"
6 colors

RattleUp
3.77" x 3.72"
2 colors

Tile
3.80" x 3.79"
5 colors

WCorner
3.01" x 3.24"
1 color

WCornerC
3.00" x 3.24"
5 colors

WHeart
3.48" x 3.49"
1 color

WHeartC
3.49" x 3.49"
7 colors

Projects & Instructions

Instructions are located on the enclosed CD-ROM.

Autograph Quilt

Bobbinwork Evening Bag

Bookworm Bag

Bookworm Bookmark

Border Belt

Box Insert

Candle Wrap

Car Shirt

Dog Mom Shirt

Dog Treat Jar

Fishbowl T-Shirt

Fringe Bag

Gumball Apron

Handmade Book

Linen Towel

Pendants

Rattle Door Hanger

Stationery

Tile Pillow

Pet Collars

Rattle Quilt

Southwest Lampshade

Wood Box

Photo Mat

Star Garland

Table Setting

Teddy Bear

Wood Tray

Resources

Contributors

The following companies supplied products featured in the book.

Accessories

Clotilde
(800) 772-2891
www.clotilde.com
Clear plates

ScrapSMART
(800) 424-1011
www.scrapsmart.com
Plastic covers, printable imagery

Sudberry House
(860) 739-6951
www.sudberry.com
Pre-finished wood products

Wisconsin Lighting
(800) 657-6999
www.wilighting.com
Hollywood Lights self-adhesive lampshades

Embroidery Designs

A Bit of Stitch, www.abitofstitch.com
Adorable Ideas, www.adorableideas.com
Amazing Designs, www.amazingdesigns.com
Anita Goodesign, www.anita-goodesign.com
A Time to Stitch, www.atimetostitch.com
Baby Lock, www.babylock.com
Bead Different Embroidery,
    www.beaddifferentembroidery.com
Bernina, www.berninausa.com

Brother, www.brothersews.com
Cactus Punch, www.cactuspunch.com
Calico Crossroads, www.calicocrossroads.com
Cindy Losekamp, www.sewingart.com
Creative Design, www.creativedesignembroidery.com
Creative Machine Embroidery, www.sewnshop.com
Criswell Embroidery & Design, www.k-lace.com
Cutting Corners, www.cuttinglinedesigns.com
Dainty Stitches, www.daintystitches.com
Dakota Collectibles, www.gonutsgocreative.com
Deb Yedziniak Smockery, smockindeb@aol.com
Decker Design Studio, www.deckerdesignstudio.com
Design By Dawn, www.designbydawn.com
Designed by Jane, www.designedbyjane.com
Designs in Stitches, www.designsinstitches.com
Embroidables, www.embroidables.com
EmbroideryArts, www.embroideryarts.com
Embroidery Central, www.embroidery.com
Embroidery Machine Essentials, www.krause.com
Embroidery Resource, www.embroideryresource.com
Hatched in Africa, www.hatchedinafrica.com
Husqvarna Viking, www.husqvarnaviking.com
Laura's Sewing Studio, www.laurassewingstudio.com
Linda Visnaw, www.lindavisnaw.com
LJI Designs, www.ljidesigns.com
Martha Pullen Company, www.marthapullen.com
Moose B Stitchin, www.moosebstitchin.net
My Embroidery Haven, www.myembroideryhaven.com
My Fair Lady Designs, www.myfairladydesigns.com
Oklahoma Embroidery Supply and Design (OESD),
    www.embroideryonline.com
Oregon Patchworks Mall, www.oregonpatchworks.com
Rowena Charlton Designs, www.rowenacharlton.com
Sadia's Designs, www.sadiasews.com
Sew Man, www.embroidery.com
Sew News, www.sewnshop.com
Singer, www.singerco.com
Smart Needle, www.smartneedle.com
Sudberry House, www.machinecrossstitch.com
Sue Lord Designs, www.suelord.com
Vermillion Stitchery, www.vsccs.com
YLI, www.ylicorp.com

Embroidery Supplies

Hoop-It-All
(800) 947-4911
www.hoopitall.com
Cover-Up vinyl topper

RNK Distributing (Floriani Products)
(877) 331-0034
www.rnkdistributing.com
Stabilizers

Sulky of America
(800) 847-4115
www.sulky.com
Puffy Foam

Magazines

Creative Machine Embroidery
(800) 677-5212
www.cmemag.com

Sew News
(800) 289-6397
www.sewnews.com

Metal

American Art Clay Co.
(317) 244-6871
www.amaco.com
Mesh and foil

Down Memory Lane
(515) 432-3222
www.quickruststeel.com
Quick Rust Steel

Notions

2-4-6-8 Pocket Bag Collection
rkb-lanett@comcast.net
Pattern

Art Institute Glitter, Inc.
(877) 909-0805
www.artglitter.com
Glitter

Blumenthal Lansing Co.
(563) 538-4243
www.buttonsplus.com
Crafter's Images CDs

The C-Thru Ruler Company
(800) 243-8419
www.cthruruler.com
Déjà Views Envelope Templates

Crafter's Pick
(510) 526-7616
www.crafterspick.com
The Ultimate! Glue

Fabric Café
(903) 509-5999
www.fabriccafe.com
Chenille Brush

Fairfield Processing Corp.
(800) 980-8000
www.poly-fil.com
Poly-fil, NU-Foam

Fiskars
(866) 348-5661
www.fiskars.com
Decorative scissors and punches

Glue Dots International
(888) 688-7131
www.gluedots.com
Glue Dots

Notions *(CONTINUED)*

Green Sneakers, Inc.
(877) 921-1015
www.greensneakers.com
Kreate-a-Lope Templates and Lick & Stick Adhesive

Kandi Corp.
(800) 985-2634
www.kandicorp.com
Kandi Kane heat-setting tool, iron-on embellishments

Klaer International
(203) 329-7001
needlethreaders@aol.com
Needle threaders

Riri Zippers
www.ririzippers.com
Decorative zippers

Silkpaint Corporation
(800) 563-0074
www.silkpaint.com
Fiber Etch

Textura Trading Company
(877) 839-8872 (877-TEXTURA)
www.texturatrading.com
Angelina Fibers

The Vintage Workshop
(913) 341-5559
www.thevintageworkshop.com
Printable imagery

Walnut Hollow Farm, Inc.
(800) 950-5101
www.walnuthollow.com
Textile Tool

The Warm Company
(800) 234-9276
www.warmcompany.com
Batting, Steam-A-Seam 2

Reference Books

"Embroidery Machine Essentials" series by
Jeanine Twigg
Krause Publications
(888) 457-2873
www.krause.com

Threads

These companies carry many different kinds of threads — only those used in book samples are listed here.

Coats & Clark
www.coatsandclark.com
Cotton, rayon, metallic, Color Twist and polyester

DMC
www.dmc-usa.com
Cotton

Madeira
www.madeirausa.com
Lana

RNK Distributing
(877) 331-0034
www.rnkdistributing.com
Floriani polyester

SolarActive International
(818) 996-8690
www.solaractiveintl.com
Solar-Reactive

Sulky of America
(800) 874-4115
www.sulky.com
12-wt. cotton, 30-wt./40-wt. rayon; invisible, UltraTwist, metallic

Wire & Rapos Threads, Inc.
(800) 937-3493
www.raposone.com
Chi-zi-mi

YLI Corp.
(803) 985-3100
www.ylicorp.com
Glow-in-the-dark, invisible, Monét, Silk Ribbon;
Specialty threads for bobbinwork (Candlelight, Designer
6, Pearl Crown Rayon, RibbonFloss)

Machines

These companies contributed the use of machines for most of the samples shown in the book (except those with a courtesy line). Note that the designs shown may be stitched on any brand of embroidery machine.

Brother International
(800) 422-7684
www.brothersews.com

Husqvarna Viking
(800) 358-0001
www.husqvarnaviking.com

Singer Sewing Co.
(800) 474-6437 (800-4-SINGER)
www.singerco.com

Software

Buzz Tools
www.buzztools.com
Buzz Size, Buzz Edit, Buzz Xplore

Kaleidoscope Collections
(970) 231-4076
www.kalcollections.com
Kaleidoscope Kreator

Wood

Midwest Products Co., Inc.
(800) 348-3497
www.midwestproducts.com

Other Resources

Atlas Gloves
www.lfsinc.com

Baby Lock
www.babylock.com

Bernina
www.berninausa.com

Elna
www.elnausa.com

Janome
www.janome.com

Kenmore
www.sears.com

Nancy's Notions
www.nancysnotions.com

Pfaff
www.pfaff.com

Prym Consumer USA
www.prymconsumerusa.com

Simplicity
www.simplicitysewing.com

Springs Creative Products Group
www.springscreativeproductsgroup.com

White
www.whitesewing.com

About the Authors

Linda Turner Griepentrog

Linda is an avid machine embroiderer and likes to challenge herself (and others) by thinking outside the hoop! She was the editor of "Sew News" magazine for 19 years and helped launch "Creative Machine Embroidery" magazine. She now owns G Wiz Creative Services and writes, edits, teaches, designs and leads tours for several companies in the sewing/craft fields. When she's not working in her home office outside Portland, Ore., she enjoys all the Northwest has to offer, especially the fabric shopping. You can reach Linda at gwizdesigns@aol.com

Rebecca Kemp Brent

Rebecca entered the world of computerized machine embroidery in 1987 with one of the first home sewing/embroidery machines available. Her enjoyment and enthusiasm have grown along with the industry. She is a freelance author, educator and designer whose work has appeared in "Creative Machine Embroidery," "Sew News" and other publications. She works from her home office in Tennessee and spends her spare time on hand needlework — and planning shopping trips to Oregon. You can reach Rebecca at rkb-lanett@comcast.net.